TWO OLD FAITHS

TWO OLD FAITHS

ESSAYS ON THE RELIGIONS OF THE HINDUS AND THE MOHAMMEDANS

BY

J. MURRAY MITCHELL, M.A., LL.D.

AND

SIR WILLIAM MUIR, LL.D., D.C.L.

GYAN

Published by

Gyan Publishing House
5, Ansari Road
Daryaganj, New Delhi-110002
Phone: 011-47034999, 9811692060
E-mail: books@gyanbooks.com

Distribution Network
gyanbooks.com
India, USA, Canada, UK, Australia, France

ISBN : 978-81-212-4175-5 (PB)
First Published, 1891

2nd Impression 2020

Printed at: Gyan Press, Delhi.

Two Old Faiths
Author: J. Murray Mitchell & Sir William Muir

TWO OLD FAITHS

ESSAYS ON THE RELIGIONS OF THE HINDUS AND THE MOHAMMEDANS

BY

J. MURRAY MITCHELL, M.A., LL.D.

AND

SIR WILLIAM MUIR, LL.D., D.C.L.

NEW YORK
CHAUTAUQUA PRESS
C. L. S. C. Department, 150 Fifth Avenue
1891

The required books of the C. L. S. C. are recommended by a Council of Six. It must, however, be understood that recommendation does not involve an approval by the Council, or by any member of it, of every principle or doctrine contained in the book recommended.

These essays have been selected from the admirable series of *Present Day Tracts*, published by the Religious Tract Society, London, and are reprinted with permission.

CONTENTS.

THE HINDU RELIGION.

OUTLINE OF THE ESSAY.

THE place of Hinduism—which is professed by about a hundred and ninety millions in India—among the religions of the world, and its great antiquity, are pointed out.

The comparative simplicity of the system contained in the Vedas, the oldest sacred books of the Hindus, its almost entire freedom from the use of images, its gradual deterioration in the later hymns, its gradual multiplication of gods, the advance of sacerdotalism, and the increasing complexity of its religious rites are set forth.

The philosophical speculation that was carried on, the different philosophical schools, the Buddhist re-action, its conflict with Brahmanism, its final defeat, and its influence on the victorious system are discussed.

The religious reconstruction represented by the Puranas, their theological character, the modern ritual, the introduction and rise of caste, and the treatment of women are then considered.

A contrast is drawn between the leading characteristics of Hinduism and those of Christianity, and the effect of Christian ideas on modern Hinduism is exhibited. The history of the Brahmo Somaj under Keshub Chunder Sen is given at some length.

THE HINDU RELIGION.

INTRODUCTION.

Hinduism deserving of study.

THE system of religious belief which is generally called Hinduism is, on many accounts, eminently deserving of study. If we desire to trace the history of the ancient religions of the widely extended Aryan or Indo-European race, to which we ourselves belong, we shall find in the earlier writings of the Hindus an exhibition of it decidedly more archaic even than that which is presented in the Homeric poems. Then, the growth—the historical development—of Hinduism is not less worthy of attention than its earlier phases. It has endured for upward of three thousand years, no doubt undergoing very important changes, yet in many things retaining its original spirit. The progress of the system has not been lawless; and it is exceedingly instructive to note the development, and, if possible, explain it.

Its antiquity.

We are, then, to endeavor to study Hinduism chronologically. Unless he does so almost every man who tries to comprehend it is, at first, overwhelmed with a feeling of utter confusion and bewilderment. Hinduism spreads out before him as a vast river, or even what seems at first

> "a dark
> Illimitable ocean, without bound,
> Without dimension, where length, breadth, and height,
> And time, and place are lost."

But matters begin to clear up when he begins at the beginning, and notes how one thing succeeded another. It may not be possible as yet to trace all the windings of the stream or to show at what precise points in its long course it was joined by such and such a tributary; yet much is known regarding the mighty river which every intelligent man will find it profitable to note and understand.

The discussion chronological.

The Christian ought not to rest satisfied with the vague general idea that Hinduism is a form of heathenism with which he has nothing to do, save to help in destroying it. Let him try to realize the ideas of the Hindu regarding God, and the soul, and sin, and salvation, and heaven, and

The Christian's duty in relation to the subject.

hell, and the many sore trials of this mortal life. He will then certainly have a much more vivid perception of the divine origin and transcendent importance of his own religion. Farther, he will then extend a helping hand to his Eastern brother with far more of sensibility and tenderness; and in proportion to the measure of his loving sympathy will doubtless be the measure of his success. A yearning heart will accomplish more than the most cogent argument.

The purpose of the Tract.

In this Tract we confine ourselves to the laying down of great leading facts and principles; but these will be dwelt upon at sufficient length to give the reader, we trust, an accurate conception of the general character and history of Hinduism. We shall also briefly contrast the system with Christianity.

The history of Hinduism may be divided into three great periods, each embracing, in round numbers, about a thousand years.

I.

THE VEDAS.

The most ancient writings of India.

REGARDING the earliest form of Hinduism we must draw our conceptions from the Veda, or, to speak more accurately, the four Vedas. The most important of these is the Rig Veda; and internal evidence proves it to be the most ancient. It contains above a thousand hymns; the earliest of which may date from about the year 1500 B. C. The Hindus, or, as they call themselves, the Aryas, had by that time entered India, and were dwelling in the north-western portion, the Panjab. The hymns, we may say, are racy of the soil. There is no reference to the life led by the people before they crossed the Himalaya Mountains or entered by some of the passes of Afghanistan.

It would be very interesting if we could discover the pre-Vedic form of the religion. Inferentially this may, to some extent, be done by comparing the teachings of the Vedas with those contained in the books of other branches of the great Aryan family—

such as the Greeks, the Romans, and, above all, the Iranians (ancient Persians).

The ancient Hindus were a highly gifted, energetic race; civilized to a considerable extent; not nomadic; chiefly shepherds and herdsmen, but also acquainted with agriculture. Commerce was not unknown; the river Indus formed a highway to the Indian Ocean, and at least the Phenicians availed themselves of it from perhaps the seventeenth century B. C., or even earlier.

The hymns are strongly religious.

As soon as we begin to study the hymns of the Veda we are struck by their strongly religious character. Tacitly assuming that the book contains the whole of the early literature of India, many writers have expressed themselves in strong terms regarding the primitive Hindus as religious above all other races.

They are a selection.

But as we read on we become convinced that these poems are a selection, rather than a collection, of the literature; and the conviction grows that the selection has been made by priestly hands for priestly purposes.

Pre-eminently sacerdotal.

An acute critic has affirmed that the Vedic poems are "pre-eminently sacerdotal, and in no sense popular."[1] We can thus

[1] Barth.

explain a pervading characteristic of the book which has taken most readers by surprise. There is a want of simplicity in the Veda. It is often most elaborate, artificial, overrefined—one might even say, affected. How could these be the thoughts, or those the expressions, of the imperfectly civilized shepherds of the Panjab? But if it be only a hymn-book, with its materials arranged for liturgical purposes, the difficulty vanishes.[1] We shall accordingly take it for granted that the Veda presents only the religious thought of the ancient Hindus—and not the whole of the religious thought, but only that of a very influential portion of the race. With all the qualifications now stated, the Veda must retain a position of high importance for all who study Indian thought and life. The religious stamp which the compilers of the Veda impressed so widely and so deeply has not been obliterated in the course of thirty centuries.

Present the religious thought of the ancient Hindus.

Their religion is Nature-worship.

The prevailing aspect of the religion presented in the Vedic hymns may be broadly designated as Nature-worship.

[1] Bergaigne, in his able treatise, *La Religion Védique*, insists earnestly on what he calls the "liturgical contamination of the myths." See vol. iii, p. 320.

Physical phenomena in India.

All physical phenomena in India are invested with a grandeur which they do not possess in northern or even southern Europe. Sunlight, moonlight, starlight, the clouds purpled with the beam of morning or flaming in the west like fiery chariots of heaven; to behold these things in their full magnificence one ought to see them in the East. Even so the sterner phenomena of nature—whirlwind and tempest, lightning and thunder, flood and storm-wave, plague, pestilence, and famine; all of these oftentimes assume in the East a character of awful majesty before which man cowers in helplessness and despair. The conceptions and feelings hence arising have from the beginning powerfully affected the religion of the Hindus. Everywhere we can trace the impress of the grander manifestations of nature—the impress of their beneficence, their beauty, their might, their mystery, or their terribleness.

Their effect on the religion.

The Sanskrit word for god is *deva*, which means *bright, shining.* Of physical phenomena it was especially those connected with light that enkindled feelings of reverence. The black thunder-cloud that enshrouded nature, in which the demon had bound the life-giving

The deities are "the bright ones," according to the language of the sacred books of India.

waters, passed away; for the glittering thunder-bolt was launched, and the streams rushed down, exulting in their freedom; and then the heaven shone out again, pure and peaceful as before. But such a wonder as the dawn—with far-streaming radiance, returning from the land of mystery, fresh in eternal youth, and scattering the terrors of the night before her—who could sufficiently admire? And let it be remembered that in the Hindu mind the interval between admiration and adoration is exceedingly small. Yet, while it is the dawn which has evoked the truest poetry, she has not retained the highest place in worship.

Fire much worshiped.

No divinity has fuller worship paid him than Agni, the Fire (*Ignis*). More hymns are dedicated to him than to any other being. Astonishment at the properties of fire; a sense of his condescension in that he, a mighty god, resides in their dwellings; his importance as the messenger between heaven and earth, bearing the offerings aloft; his kindness at night in repelling the darkness and the demons which it hides—all these things raised Agni to an exalted place. He is fed with pure clarified butter, and so rises heavenward in his brightness. The physical conception of fire, however, adheres to him, and he never quite ceases to be the earthly flame; yet mystical conceptions thickly gather round this root-idea; he is fire pervading all nature; and he often becomes supreme, a god of gods.

Soma highly exalted.

All this seems natural enough; but one is hardly prepared for the high exaltation to which Soma is raised. Soma is properly the juice of a milky plant (*asclepias acida*, or *sarcostemma viminale*), which, when fermented, is intoxicating. The simple-minded Aryas were both astonished and delighted at its effects; they liked it themselves; and they knew nothing more precious to present to their gods. Accordingly, all of these rejoice in it. Indra in particular quaffs it "like a thirsty stag;" and under its exhilarating effects he strides victoriously to battle. Soma itself becomes a god, and a very mighty one; he is even the creator and father of the gods;[1] the king of gods and men;[2] all creatures are in his hand.

Soma becomes a very mighty god.

It is surely extraordinary that the Aryas could apply such hyperbolical laudations to the liquor which they had made to trickle into the vat, and which they knew to be the juice of a plant they had cut down on the mountains and pounded in a mortar; and that intoxication should be confounded with inspiration. Yet

[1] R. V., ix, 42, 4. [2] R. V., ix, 97, 24.

of such aberrations we know the human mind is perfectly capable.

Connection with Persian, Greek, and Roman systems.

We have first referred to Agni and Soma, as being the only divinities of highest rank which still retain their physical character. The worship paid to them was of great antiquity; for it is also prescribed in the Persian Avesta, and must have been common to the Indo-Iranian branch of the Aryan race before the Hindus entered India. But we can inferentially go still further back and speak of a deity common to the Greeks, Romans, Persians, and Hindus.

Varuna, the god of heaven.

This deity is Varuna, the most remarkable personality in the Veda. The name, which is etymologically connected with Οὐρανός, signifies "the encompasser," and is applied to heaven—especially the all-encompassing, extreme vault of heaven—not the nearer sky, which is the region of cloud and storm.

The sublimity of the Vedic description of him.

It is in describing Varuna that the Veda rises to the greatest sublimity which it ever reaches. A mysterious presence, a mysterious power, a mysterious knowledge amounting almost to omniscience, are ascribed to Varuna. The winkings of men's eyes are numbered by him. He upholds order, both physical and moral, throughout the universe.

The winds are his breath, the sun his eye, the sky his garment. He rewards the good and punishes the wicked. Yet to the truly penitent he is merciful. It is absolutely confounding to pass from a hymn that celebrates the serene majesty and awful purity of Varuna to one filled with measureless laudations of Soma or Agni. Could conceptions of divinity so incongruous co-exist? That they could not spring up in the same mind, or even in the same age, is abundantly manifest. And, as we have mentioned, the loftier conceptions of divinity are unquestionably the earlier. It is vain to speak, as certain writers do, of religion gradually refining itself, as a muddy stream can run itself pure; Hinduism resembles the Ganges, which, when it breaks forth from its mountain cradle at Hardwar, is comparatively pellucid, but, as it rolls on, becomes more and more muddy, discolored, and unclean.[1]

Contrast with the laudations of Agni and Soma.

The loftier conceptions of divinity the earlier.

Various scholars affirm that Varuna, in more an-

[1] The religion of the Indo-European race, while still united, "recognized a supreme God; an organizing God; almighty, omniscient, moral. . . . This conception was a heritage of the past. . . . The supreme God was originally the God of heaven." So Darmesteter, *Contemporary Review*, October, 1879. Roth had previously written with much learning and acuteness to the same effect.

cient, pre-Vedic times, held a position still higher than the very high one which he still retains. This is probable; indeed, it is certain that, before later divinities had intruded, he held a place of unrivaled majesty. But, in the Vedas, Indra is a more conspicuous figure. He corresponds to the Jupiter Pluvius of the Romans. In north-western India, after the burning heat, the annual return of the rains was hailed with unspeakable joy; it was like life succeeding death. The clouds that floated up from the ocean were at first thin and light; ah! a hostile demon was in them, carrying off the healing waters and not permitting them to fall; but the thunder-bolt of Indra flashed; the demon was driven away howling, and the emancipated streams refreshed the thirsty earth. Varuna was not indeed dethroned, but he was obscured, by the achievements of the warlike Indra; and the supersensuous, moral conceptions that were connected with the former gradually faded from the minds of the people, and Varuna erelong became quite a subordinate figure in the Pantheon.

Indra.

His achievements.

Number and relations of deities uncertain.

The deities are generally said in the Veda to be "thrice eleven" in number. We also hear of three thousand three hundred and thirty-nine. There is no *system*, no fixed order in the hierarchy; a deity who in one hymn is quite subordinate becomes in another supreme; almost every god becomes supreme in turn; in one hymn he is the son of some deity and in another that deity's father, and so (if logic ruled) his own grandfather. Every poet exalts his favorite god, till the mind becomes utterly bewildered in tracing the relationships.

We have already spoken of Agni, Varuna, and Indra, as well as Soma. Next to these in importance may come the deities of light, namely, the sun, the dawn, and the two Asvina or beams that accompany the dawn. The winds come next. The earth is a goddess. The waters are goddesses. It is remarkable that the stars are very little mentioned; and the moon holds no distinguished place.

Hardly any fetichism in the Rig Veda.

In the religion of the Rig Veda we hardly see fetichism—if by fetichism we mean the worship of small physical objects, such as stones, shells, plants, etc., which are believed to be charged (so to speak) with divinity, though this appears in the fourth Veda—the Atharva. But even in the Rig Veda almost any object that is grand, beneficent, or terrible may be adored; and implements associated with worship are themselves worshiped.

Thus, the war-chariot, the plow, the furrow, etc., are prayed to.

Early tendency toward pantheism.

A pantheistic conception of nature was also present in the Indian mind from very early times, although its development was later. Even in the earliest hymns any portion of nature with which man is brought into close relation may be adored.[1]

Reverence of the dead.

We must on no account overlook the reverence paid to the dead. The *pitris* (*patres*) or fathers are frequently referred to in the Veda. They are clearly distinguished from the *devas* or gods. In later writings they are also distinguished from men, as having been created separately from them; but this idea does not appear in the Veda. Yama, the first mortal, traveled the road by which none returns, and now drinks the Soma in the innermost of heaven, surrounded by the other fathers. These come also, along with the gods, to the banquets prepared for them on earth, and, sitting on the sacred grass, rejoice in the exhilarating draught.

The subjects of the hymns of the Rig Veda.

The hymns of the Rig Veda celebrate the power, exploits, or generosity of the deity invoked, and sometimes his personal beauty.

[1] Muir's *Sanskrit Texts*, v, 412.

The praises lavished on the god not only secured his favor but increased his power to help the worshiper.

The holiest prayer.

There is one prayer (so called) which is esteemed pre-eminently holy; generally called—from the meter in which it is composed—the Gayatri.[1] It may be rendered thus:

> "Let us meditate on that excellent glory of the Divine Son (or Vivifier); may he enlighten our understandings!"

It has always been frequently repeated in important rites.

Atharva Veda.

So far we have referred almost exclusively to the Rig Veda. The next in importance is the Atharva, sometimes termed the Brahma Veda; which we may render the Veda of incantations. It contains six hundred and seventy hymns. Of these a few are equal to those in the Rig Veda; but, as a whole, the Atharva is far inferior to the other in a moral and spiritual point of view. It abounds in imprecations, charms for the destruction of enemies, and so forth. Talismans, plants, or gems are invoked, as possessed of irresistible might to kill or heal. The deities are often different from those of the Rig Veda. The Atharva

Inferior morally and spiritually to the Rig Veda.

[1] R. V., iii, 62, 10.

manifests a great dread of malignant beings, whose wrath it deprecates. We have thus simple demon-worship. How is this great falling-off to be explained? In one of two ways. Either a considerable time intervened between the composition of the two books, during which the original faith had rapidly degenerated, probably through contact with aboriginal races who worshiped dark and sanguinary deities; or else there had existed from the beginning two forms of the religion—the higher of which is embodied in the hymns of the Rig Veda, and the lower in the Atharva. We believe the latter explanation to be correct, although doubtless the superstitions of the aborigines must all along have exerted an influence on the faith of the invaders.

Explanation of deterioration.

The offerings.

The offerings presented to the gods consisted chiefly of clarified butter, curdled milk, rice-cakes, and fermented Soma juice, which was generally mixed with water or milk. All was thrown into the fire, which bore them or their essences to the gods. The Soma was also sprinkled on the sacred grass, which was strewn on the floor, and on which the gods and fathers were invited to come and seat themselves that they might enjoy the cheering beverage. The remainder was drunk by the officiating priests. The offerings were understood to nourish and gratify the gods as corporeal beings.

Animal victims.

Animal victims are also offered up. We hear of sheep, goats, bulls, cows, and buffaloes being sacrificed, and sometimes in large numbers. But the great offering was the Asvamedha, or sacrifice of the horse. The body of the horse was hacked to pieces; the fragments were dressed—part was boiled, part roasted; some of the flesh was then eaten by the persons present, and the rest was offered to the gods. Tremendous was the potency—at least as stated in later times—of a hundred such sacrifices; it rendered the offerer equal or superior to the gods; even the mighty Indra trembled for his sovereignty and strove to hinder the consummation of the awful rite.

Human sacrifice.

Human sacrifice was not unknown, though there are very few allusions to it in the earlier hymns.

Sacrifice deemed of very high importance.

Even from the first, however, the rite of sacrifice occupies a very high place, and allusions to it are exceedingly frequent. The observances connected with it are said to be the "first religious rites." Sacrifice was early believed to be expiatory; it removed sin. It was substitutionary; the victim stood in place of the offerer. All order in the universe depends upon it; it is "the nave of the world-wheel." Sometimes Vishnu is said to be the sacrifice; sometimes even the Supreme Being himself is so. Elaborated ideas and a complex ritual, which we could have expected to grow up only in the course of ages, appear from very early times. We seem compelled to draw the inference that sacrifice formed an essential and very important part of the pre-Vedic faith.[1]

In the Veda worship is a kind of barter. In exchange for praises and offerings the deity is asked to bestow favors. Temporal blessings are implored, such as food, wealth, life, children, cows, horses, success in battle, the destruction of enemies, and so forth. Not much is said regarding sin and the need of forgiveness. A distinguished scholar[2] has said that "the religious notion of sin is wanting altogether;" but this affirmation is decidedly too sweeping.

No image-worship.

The worship exemplified in the Veda is not image-worship. Images of the fire, or the winds, or the waters could hardly be required,

[1] The rites, says Haug, "must have existed from times immemorial." —*Aitareya Brâhmana*, pp. 7, 9.

[2] Weber, *History of Indian Literature*, p. 38.

and while the original nature-worship lasted, idols must have been nearly unknown. Yet the description of various deities is so precise and full that it seems to be probably drawn from visible representations of them. Worship was personal and domestic, not in any way public. Indeed, two men praying at the same time had to pray quite apart, so that neither might disturb the other. Each dealt with heaven, so to speak, solely on his own behalf.

No public worship.

We hear of no places set apart as temples in Vedic times.

No temples.

A Veda consists of two parts called *Mantra* or *Sanhita*, and *Brahmana*. The first is composed of hymns. The second is a statement of ritual, and is generally in prose. The existing Brahmanas are several centuries later than the great body of the hymns, and were probably composed when the Hindus had crossed the Indus, and were advancing along the Gangetic valley. The oldest may be about the date of 800 or 700 B. C.

The treatises on ritual.

The Brahmanas are very poor, both in thought and expression. They have hardly their match in any literature for "pedantry and downright absurdity."[1] Poetical feeling and even religious feeling seem

[1] Max Müller, *Ancient Sanskrit Literature*, p. 389.

gone; all is dead and dry as dust. By this time the Sanskrit language had ceased to be generally understood. The original texts could hardly receive accessions; the most learned man could do little more than interpret, or perhaps misinterpret, them. The worshiper looked on; he worshiped now by proxy. Thus the priest had risen greatly in importance. He alone knew the sacred verses and the sacred rites. An error in the pronunciation of the mystic text might bring destruction on the worshiper; what could he do but lean upon the priest? The latter could say the prayers if he could not pray. All this worked powerfully for the elevation of the Brahmans, the "men of prayer;" they steadily grew into a class, a caste; and into this no one could enter who was not of priestly descent. Schools were now found necessary for the study of the sacred books, rites, and traditions. The importance which these attach to theology—doctrine—is very small; the externals of religion are all in all. The rites, in fact, now threw the very gods into the shade; every thing depended on their due performance. And thus the Hindu ritual gradually grew up into a stupendous system, the most elaborate, complex, and burdensome which the earth has seen.

Growth of priestly power.

Schools for the study of sacred books, rites, and traditions.

Moral character of the Veda.

It is time, however, to give a brief estimate of the moral character of the Veda. The first thing that strikes us is its inconsistency. Some hymns—especially those addressed to Varuna—rise as high as Gentile conceptions regarding deity ever rose; others—even in the Rig Veda—sink miserably low; and in the Atharva we find, "even in the lowest depth, a lower still."

Indra supersedes Varuna.

The character of Indra—who has displaced or overshadowed Varuna[1]—has no high attributes. He is "voracious;" his "inebriety is most intense;" he "dances with delight in battle." His worshipers supply him abundantly with the drink he loves; and he supports them against their foes, ninety and more of whose cities he has destroyed. We do not know that these foes, the Dasyus, were morally worse than the intrusive Aryas, but the feelings of the latter toward the former were of unexampled ferocity. Here is one passage out of multitudes similar:

> "Hurl thy hottest thunder-bolt upon them! Uproot them! Cleave them asunder! O, Indra, overpower, subdue, slay the demon! Pluck him up! Cut him through the middle! Crush his head!"

Indra, if provided with Soma, is always indulgent

[1] "The haughty Indra takes precedence of all gods." R. V., l, 55.

to his votaries; he supports them *per fas et nefas*.

Deterioration begins early.

Varuna, on the other hand, is grave, just, and to wicked men severe.[1] The supersession of Varuna by Indra, then, is easily understood. We see the principle on which it rests stated in the Old Testament. "Ye cannot serve the Lord," said Joshua to the elders of Israel; "for he is a holy God." Even so Jeremiah points sorrowfully to the fact that the pagan nations clung to their false gods, while Israel was faithless to the true. As St. Paul expresses it, "they did not like to retain God in their knowledge." Unless this principle is fully taken into account we cannot understand the historical development of Hinduism.

Varuna the only divinity possessed of pure and elevated attributes.

The Veda frequently ascribes to the gods, to use the language of Max Müller, "sentiments and passions unworthy of deity." In truth, except in the case of Varuna, there is not one divinity that is possessed of pure and elevated attributes.

[1] "These two personages [Indra and Varuna] sum up the two conceptions of divinity, between which the religious consciousness of the Vedic Aryans seems to oscillate."—Bergaigne, *La Religion Védique*, vol. iii, p. 149.

II.

PHILOSOPHY, AND RITUALISM.

Speculation begins.

During the Vedic period—certainly toward its conclusion—a tendency to speculation had begun to appear. Probably it had all along existed in the Hindu mind, but had remained latent during the stirring period when the people were engaged in incessant wars. Climate, also, must have affected the temperament of the race; and, as the Hindus steadily pressed down the valley of the Ganges into warmer regions, their love of repose and contemplative quietism would continually deepen. And when the Brahmans became a fully developed hierarchy, lavishly endowed, with no employment except the performance of religious ceremonies, their minds could avoid stagnation only by having recourse to speculative thought.

Rise of asceticism.

Again, asceticism has a deep root in human nature; earnest souls, conscious of their own weakness, will fly from the temptations of the world. Various causes thus led numbers of men to seek a life of seclusion; they dwelt chiefly in forests, and there they revolved the everlasting problems of existence, creation, the soul, and God. The lively Greeks, for whom, with all their high intellectual endowments, a happy sensuous existence was nearly all in all, were amazed at the numbers in northern India who appeared weary of the world and indifferent to life itself. By and for these recluses were gradually composed the Aranyakas, or forest treatises; and out of these grew a series of more regular works, called Upanishads.[1] At least two hundred and fifty of these are known to exist. They have been called "guesses at truth;" they are more so than formal solutions of great questions. Many of them are unintelligible rhapsodies; others rise almost to sublimity. They frequently contradict each other; the same writer sometimes contradicts himself. One prevailing characteristic is all-important; their doctrine is pantheism. The pantheism is sometimes not so much a coldly reasoned system as an aspiration, a yearning, a deep-felt need of something better than the mob of gods who came in the train of Indra, and the darker deities who were still crowding in. Even in spite of

Upanishads.

They are pantheistic.

[1] The meaning of the term is not quite certain. *Sessions*, or *Instructions*, may perhaps be the rendering. So Monier Williams.

the counteracting power of the Gospel mysticism has run easily into pantheism in Europe, and orthodox Christians sometimes slide unconsciously into it, or at least into its language.[1] But, as has been already noted, a strain of pantheism existed in the Hindu mind from early times.

Accordingly, these hermit sages, these mystic dreamers, soon came to identify the human soul with God. And the chief end of man was to seek that the stream derived from God should return to its source, and, ceasing to wander through the wilderness of this world, should find repose in the bosom of the illimitable deep, the One, the All. The Brahmans attached the Upanishads to the Veda proper, and they soon came to be regarded as its most sacred part. In this way the influence these treatises have exercised has been immense; more than any other portion of the earlier Hindu writings they have molded the thoughts of succeeding generations. Philosophy had thus begun.

The speculations of which we see the commence-

[1] For example, Wordsworth:

"Thou, Thou alone
Art everlasting, and the blessed Spirits
Which Thou includest, as the sea her waves."
—*Excursion*, book iv.

ment and progress in the Upanishads were finally developed and classified in a series of writings called the six Sastras or *darsanas*. These constitute the regular official philosophy of India. They are without much difficulty reducible to three leading schools of thought—the Nyaya, the Sankhya, and the Vedanta.

Six philosophic schools.

Roundly, and speaking generally, we may characterize these systems as theistic, atheistic, and pantheistic respectively.

The Nyaya.

It is doubtful, however, whether the earlier form of the Nyaya was theistic or not. The later form is so, but it says nothing of the moral attributes of God, nor of his government. The chief end of man, according to the Nyaya, is deliverance from pain; and this is to be attained by cessation from all action, whether good or bad.

The Sankhya.

The Sankhya declares matter to be self-existent and eternal. Soul is distinct from matter, and also eternal. When it attains true knowledge it is liberated from matter and from pain. The Sankhya holds the existence of God to be without proof.

But the leading philosophy of India is unquestionably the Vedanta. The name means "the end or scope of the Veda;" and if the Upanishads were the Veda, instead of treatises tacked on to it, the name would be correct; for the Vedanta, like the Upanishads, inculcates pantheism.

The Vedanta.

The form which this philosophy ultimately assumed is well represented in the treatise called the Vedanta Sara, or essence of the Vedanta. A few extracts will suffice to exhibit its character. "The unity of the soul and God—this is the scope of all Vedanta treatises." We have frequent references made to the "great saying," *Tat twam*—that is, That art thou, or Thou art God; and *Aham Brahma*, that is, I am God. Again it is said, "The whole universe is God." God is "existence (or more exactly an existent thing[1]), knowledge, and joy." Knowledge, not a knower; joy, not one who rejoices.

Every thing else has only a seeming existence, which is in consequence of ignorance (or illusion). Ignorance makes the soul think itself different from God; and it also "projects" the appearance of an external world.

It teaches absolute idealism.

"He who knows God becomes God." "When He, the first and last, is discerned, one's own acts are annihilated."

[1] Or, the thing that really is—the ὄντως ὄν.

Meditation, without distinction of subject and object, is the highest form of thought. It is a high attainment to say, "I am God;" but the consummation is when thought exists without an object.

There are four states of the soul—waking, dreaming, dreamless sleep, and the "fourth state," or pure intelligence. The working-man is in dense ignorance; in sleep he is freed from part of this ignorance; in dreamless sleep he is freed from still more; but the consummation is when he attains something beyond this, which it seems cannot be explained, and is therefore called the fourth state.

Doctrine of "the Self."

The name, which in later writings is most frequently given to the "one without a second,"[1] is Atman, which properly means self. Much is said of the way in which the self in each man is to recover, or discover, its unity with the supreme or real self. For as the one sun shining in the heavens is reflected, often in distorted images, in multitudes of vessels filled with water, so the one self is present in all human minds.[2] There is not—perhaps there could not be—consistency in the state-

[1] *Ekamadvitiyam.*

[2] This illustration is in the mouth of every Hindu disputant at the present day.

ments of the relation of the seeming to the real. In most of the older books a practical or conventional existence is admitted of the self in each man, but not a real existence. But when the conception is fully formulated the finite world is not admitted to exist save as a mere illusion. All phenomena are a play—a play without plot or purpose, which the absolute plays with itself.[1] This is surely transcendent transcendentalism. One regrets that speculation did not take one step more, and declare that the illusion was itself illusory. Then we should have gone round the circle, and returned to *sensus communis.* We must be pardoned if we seem to speak disrespectfully of such fantastic speculations; we desire rather to speak regretfully of the many generations of men which successively occupied themselves with such unprofitable dreams; for this kind of thought is traceable even from Vedic days. It is more fully developed in the Upanishads. In them occurs the classical sentence so frequently quoted in later literature, which declares that the absolute being is the "one [thing] without a second."[2]

Inconsistent statements.

The book which perhaps above all others has molded the mind of India in more recent days is

[1] Barth, p. 75. [2] *Ekamadvitiyam.*

the Bhagavad Gita, or Song of the Holy One. It is written in stately and harmonious verse, and has achieved the same task for Indian philosophy as Lucretius did for ancient Epicureanism.[1] It is eclectic, and succeeds, in a sort of way, in forcing the leading systems of Indian thought into seeming harmony.

The Gita.

Some have thought they could discern in these daring speculations indications of souls groping after God, and saddened because of the difficulty of finding him. Were it so, all our sympathies would at once be called forth. But no; we see in these writings far more of intellectual pride than of spiritual sadness. Those ancient dreamers never learned their own ignorance. They scarcely recognized the limitations of the human mind. And when reason could take them no farther they supplemented it by dreams and ecstasy until, in the Yoga philosophy, they rushed into systematized mysticisms and magic far more extravagant than the wildest *theurgy* of the degraded Neoplatonism of the Roman Empire.

Intellectual pride.

[1] Volui tibi suaviloquenti
Carmine Pierio rationem exponere nostram
Et quasi Musæo dulci contingere melle.

A learned writer thus expresses himself:

> "The only one of the six schools that seem to recognize the doctrine of divine providence is the Yoga. It thus seems that the consistent followers of these systems can have, in their perfected state, no religion, no action, and no moral character."[1]

Indian philosophy a sad failure.

And now to take a brief review of the whole subject. The Hindu sages were men of acute and patient thought; but their attempt to solve the problem of the divine and human natures, of human destiny and duty, has ended in total failure. Each system baseless, and all mutually conflicting; systems cold and cheerless, that frown on love and virtuous exertion, and speak of annihilation or its equivalent, absorption, as our highest hope: such is the poor result of infinite speculation. "The world by wisdom knew not God." O, that India would learn the much-needed lesson of humility which the experience of ages ought to teach her!

Sacerdotalism.

While speculation was thus busy Sacerdotalism was also continually extending its influence. The Brahman, the man of prayer, had made himself indispensable in all sacred rites. He alone—as we have seen—knew the holy text; he alone could rightly pronounce the words of awful mystery and

[1] Dr. J. Muir, in *North British Review*, No. xlix, p. 224.

power on which depended all weal or woe. On all religious occasions the priest must be called in, and, on all occasions, implicitly obeyed. For a considerable time the princes struggled against the encroachments of the priests; but in the end they were completely vanquished. Never was sacerdotal tyranny more absolute; the proudest pope in mediæval times never lorded it over Western Christendom with such unrelenting rigor as the Brahmans exercised over both princes and people. The feeling of the priests is expressed in a well-known stanza:

The tyranny of sacerdotalism.

> "All the world is subject to the gods; the gods are subject to the holy texts; the holy texts are subject to the Brahman; therefore the Brahman is my god."

Yes, the sacred man could breathe the spell which made earth and hell and heaven itself to tremble. He therefore logically called himself an earthly god. Indeed, the Brahman is always logical. He draws conclusions from premises with iron rigor of reasoning; and with side-issues he has nothing to do. He stands upon his rights. Woe to the being—god or man—who comes in conflict with him!

Ritual becomes extravagant.

The priests naturally multiplied religious ceremonies, and made ritual the soul of worship. Sacrifice especially assumed still more and more exaggerated forms—becoming more protracted, more expensive, more bloody. A hecatomb of victims was but a small offering. More and more awful powers were ascribed to the rite.

Reaction.

But the tension was too great, and the bow snapped. Buddhism arose. We may call this remarkable system the product of the age—an inevitable rebellion against intolerable sacerdotalism; and yet we must not overlook the importance of the very distinct and lofty personality of Buddha (Sakya Muni) as a power molding it into shape.

Buddhism.

Wherever it extended it effected a vast revolution in Indian thought. Thus in regard to the institution of caste, Buddha did not attack it; he did not, it would appear, even formally renounce it; as a mere social institution he seems to have acknowledged it; but then he held that all the *religious* were freed from its restrictions. "My law," said he, "is a law of mercy for all;" and forthwith he proceeded to admit men of every caste into the closest fellowship with himself and his followers. Then, he preached—he, though not a Brahman—in the vernacular languages—an immense innovation, which made his teachings popular. He put in the forefront of his system certain great fundamental principles of morality. He made religion consist in duty, not rites. He reduced duty mainly to mercy or kindness toward all living beings—a marvelous generalization. This set aside all slaughter of animals. The mind of the princes and people was weary of priestcraft and ritualism; and the teaching of the great reformer was most timely. Accordingly his doctrine spread with great rapidity, and for a long time it seemed likely to prevail over Brahmanism. But various causes gradually combined against it. Partly, it was overwhelmed by its own luxuriance of growth; partly, Brahmanism, which had all along maintained an intellectual superiority, adopted, either from conviction or policy, most of the principles of Buddhism, and skillfully supplied some of its main deficiencies. Thus the Brahmans retained their position; and, at least nominally, their religion won the day.

Moral elements of this system.

Conflict with Brahmanism.

Victory of Brahmanism.

III.

RECONSTRUCTION—MODERN HINDUISM.

Revival, in an altered form, of Hinduism.

But the Hinduism that grew up, as Buddhism faded from Indian soil, was widely different from the system with which early Buddhism had contended. Hinduism, as it has been developed during the last thousand or twelve hundred years, resembles a stupendous far-extended building, or series of buildings, which is still receiving additions, while portions have crumbled and are crumbling into ruin. Every conceivable style of architecture, from that of the stately palace to the meanest hut, is comprehended in it. On a portion of the structure here or there the eye may rest with pleasure; but as a whole it is an unsightly, almost monstrous, pile. Or, dismissing figures, we must describe it as the most extraordinary creation which the world has seen. A jumble of all things; polytheistic pantheism; much of Buddhism; something apparently of Christianity, but terribly disfigured; a science wholly outrageous; shreds of history twisted into wild mythology; the bold poetry of the older books understood as literal prose; any local deity, any demon of the aborigines, however hideous, identified with some accredited Hindu divinity; any custom, however repugnant to common sense or common decency, accepted and explained—in a word, later Hinduism has been omnivorous; it has partially absorbed and assimilated every system of belief, every form of worship, with which it has come in contact. Only to one or two things has it remained inflexibly true. It has steadily upheld the proudest pretensions of the Brahman; and it has never relaxed the sternest restrictions of caste. We cannot wonder at the severe judgment pronounced on Hinduism by nearly every Western author. According to Macaulay, "all is hideous and grotesque and ignoble;" and the calmer De Tocqueville maintains that "Hinduism is perhaps the only system of belief that is worse than having no religion at all."[1]

Only the position of the Brahman and the restrictions of caste retained.

When a modern Hindu is asked what are the sacred books of his religion he generally answers: "The Vedas, the Sastras (that is, philosophical systems), and the Puranas." Some authorities add the Tantras.

[1] *Miscellaneous Writings* (Macmillan, 1861), vol. i, p. 77.

The modern form of Hinduism is exhibited chiefly in the eighteen Puranas, and an equal number of Upapuranas (minor Puranas).[1]

The Puranas.

When we compare the religion embodied in the Puranas with that of Vedic times we are startled at the magnitude of the change. The Pantheon is largely new; old deities have been superseded; other deities have taken their place. There has been both accretion from without and evolution from within. The thirty-three gods of the Vedas have been fantastically raised to three hundred and thirty millions. Siva, Durga, Rama, Krishna, Kali—unknown in ancient days—are now mighty divinities; Indra is almost entirely overlooked, and Varuna has been degraded from his lofty throne and turned into a regent of the waters.

New deities, rites, and customs.

The worship of the Linga (phallus) has been introduced. So has the great dogma of Transmigration, which has stamped a deeper impress on later Hindu mind than almost any other doctrine. Caste is fully established, though in Vedic days scarcely, if at all, recognized. The dreadful prac-

[1] But the truth is that every man is accounted a good Hindu who keeps the rules of caste and pays due respect to the Brahmans. What he believes, or disbelieves, is of little or no consequence.

tice of widow-burning has been brought in, and this by a most daring perversion of the Vedic texts. Woman, in fact, has fallen far below the position assigned her in early days.

The Trimurtti, a triad of gods.

One of the notable things in connection with the reconstruction of Hinduism is the position it gives to the Trimurtti, or triad of gods—Brahma, Vishnu, and Siva. Something like an anticipation of this has been presented in the later Vedic times: fire, air, and the sun (Agni, Vayu, and Surya) being regarded by the commentator[1] as summing up the divine energies. But in the Vedas the deities often go in pairs; and little stress should be laid on the idea of a Vedic triad. That idea, however, came prominently forward in later days. The worship both of Vishnu and Siva may have existed, from ancient times, as popular rites not acknowledged by the Brahmans; but both of these deities were now fully recognized. The god Brahma was an invention of the Brahmans; he was no real divinity of the people, and had hardly ever been actually worshiped. It is usual to designate Brahma, Vishnu, and Siva as Creator, Preserver, and Destroyer respectively; but the generalization is by no means well maintained in the Hindu books.

[1] Yaska, probably in the fifth century B. C.

The Puranas are in general violently sectarian; some being Vishnuite, others Sivite. It is in connection with Vishnu, especially, that the idea of incarnation becomes prominent. The Hindu term is *Avatara*, literally, *descent;* the deity is represented as descending from heaven to earth, for vindication of the truth and righteousness, or, to use the words ascribed to Krishna,

The Avatara.

For the preservation of the good, and the destruction of the wicked,
For the establishment of religion, I am born from age to age.

The "descents" of Vishnu are usually reckoned ten. Of these by far the most celebrated are those of Rama and Krishna. The great importance attached to these two deities has been traced to the influence of Buddhism. That system had exerted immense power in consequence of the gentle and attractive character ascribed to Buddha. The older gods were dim, distant, and often stern; some near, intelligible, and loving divinity was longed for. Buddha was a brother-man, and yet a quasi-deity; and hearts longing for sympathy and succor were strongly attracted by such a personality.

The "descents" of Vishnu.

The character of Rama—or Ramachandra—is possessed of some high qualities. The great poem in which it is described at fullest length—the Ramayana of Valmiki—seems to have been an alteration, made in the interests of Hinduism, of early Buddhist legends; and the Buddhist quality of gentleness has not disappeared in the history.[1] Rama, however, is far from a perfect character. His wife Sita is possessed of much womanly grace and every wifely virtue; and the sorrowful story of the warrior-god and his faithful spouse has appealed to deep sympathies in the human breast. The worship of Rama has seldom, if ever, degenerated into lasciviousness. In spite, however, of the charm thrown around the life of Rama and Sita by the genius of Valmiki and Tulsida,[2] it is Krishna, not Rama, that has attained the greatest popularity among the "descents" of Vishnu.

The god Rama.

Very different morally from that of Rama is the character of Krishna. While Rama is but a partial manifestation of divinity Krishna is a full manifestation; yet what a manifestation! He is represented as full of naughty tricks in his youth, although exercising the highest powers

Krishna.

[1] Weber thinks that Christian elements may have been introduced, in course of time, into the representation.

[2] His Ramayana was written in Hindi verse in the sixteenth century.

of deity; and, when he grows up, his conduct is grossly immoral and disgusting. It is most startling to think that this being is by grave writers—like the authors of the Bhagavad Gita and the Bhagavata Purana—made the highest of the gods, or, indeed, the only real God. Stranger still, if possible, is the probability that the early life of Krishna—in part, at least—is a dreadful travesty of the early life of Christ, as given in the apocryphal gospels, especially the Gospel of the Infancy. The falling off in the apocryphal gospels, when compared with the canonical, is truly sad; but the falling off even from the apocryphal ones, in the Hindu books, is altogether sickening.[1]

His early life a travesty of the life of Christ, according to the Gospel of the Infancy.

A very striking characteristic of modern Hinduism is what is termed *bhakti*, or devotion. There are three great ways of attaining to salvation: *karma marga*, or the way of ceremonial works; *jnana*

[1] When Jhansi was captured in the times of the great mutiny English officers were disgusted to see the walls of the queen's palace covered with what they described as "grossly obscene" pictures. There is little or no doubt that these were simply representations of the acts of Krishna. Therefore to the Hindu queen they were religious pictures. When questioned about such things the Brahmans reply that deeds which would be wicked in men were quite right in Krishna, who, being God, could do whatever he pleased.

marga, or the way of knowledge, and *bhakti marga*, or the way of devotion.

Doctrine of *bhakti* introduced.

The notion of trust in the gods was familiar to the mind of India from Vedic days, but the deity was indistinct and unsympathetic, and there could hardly be love and attachment to him. But there now arose the doctrine of *bhakti* (devotion), which resolved religion into emotion. It came into the Hindu system rather abruptly; and many learned men have traced its origin to the influence of Christianity. This is quite possible; but perhaps the fact is hardly proved. Contact with Christianity, however, probably accelerated a process which had previously begun.

Influence of the system.

At all events, the system of *bhakti* has had, and still has, great sway in India, particularly in Bengal, among the followers of Chaitanya, and the large body of people in western India who style themselves *Vaishnavas* or *Bhaktas* (devotees). The popular poetry of Maharashtra, as exemplified in such poets as Tukarama, is an impassioned inculcation of devotion to Vithoba of Pandharpur, who is a manifestation of Krishna.

Mixed with Buddhist elements.

Into the *bhakti* system of western India Buddhist elements have entered; and the school of devotees is often denominated Bauddha-Vaishnava. Along with extravagant idolatry it inculcates generally, at least in the Maratha country, a pure morality; and the latter it apparently owes to Buddhism. Yet there are many sad lapses from purity. Almost of necessity the worship of Krishna led to corruption. The hymns became erotic; and movements hopeful at their commencement—like that of Chaitanya of Bengal, in the sixteenth century —soon grievously fell off in character. The attempt to make religion consist of emotion without thought, of *bhakti* without *jnana*, had disastrous issues. Coincident with the development of *bhakti* was the exaltation of the *guru*, or religious teacher, which soon amounted to deification—a change traceable from about the twelfth century A. D.

Exaltation of the *guru*.

When pressed on the subject of Krishna's evil deeds many are anxious to explain them as allegorical representations of the union between the divinity and true worshipers; but some interpret them in the most literal way possible. This is done especially by the followers of Vallabha Acharya.[1] These men attained a most unenviable notoriety about twenty years ago, when a case was tried

Explanations of Krishna's evil deeds.

[1] Born probably in 1649.

in the Supreme Court of Bombay, which revealed the practice of the most shameful licentiousness by the religious teachers and their female followers, and this as a part of worship! The disgust excited was so great and general that it was believed the influence of the sect was at an end; but this hope unhappily has not been realized.

Reforms attempted.

Reformers have arisen from time to time in India; men who saw the deplorable corruption of religion, and strove to restore it to what they considered purity. Next to Buddha we may mention Kabir, to whom are ascribed many verses still popular.

Kabir.

Probably the doctrine of the unity of God, as maintained by the Mohammedans, had impressed him. He opposed idolatry, caste, and Brahmanical assumption. Yet his monotheism was a kind of pantheism. His date may be the beginning of the fifteenth century.

Nanak.

Nanak followed and founded the religion of the Sikhs. His sacred book, the *Granth*, is mainly pantheistic; it dwells earnestly on devotion, especially devotion to the *guru*. The Sikhs now seem slowly relapsing into idolatry. In truth, the history of all attempts at reformation in India has been most discouragiug. Sect after sect has successively risen to some elevation above the prevalent idolatry; and then gradually, as by some irresistible gravitation, it has sunk back into the *mare magnum* of Hinduism. If we regard experience, purification from within is hopeless; the struggle for it is only a repetition of the toil of Sisyphus, and always with the same sad issue. Deliverance must come from without—from the Gospel of Jesus Christ.

Failure of all reforms.

We mentioned the Tantras as exerting great influence in later days.[1] In these the worship of Siva, and, still more, that of his wife, is predominant. The deity is now supposed to possess a double nature—one quiescent, one active; the latter being regarded as the *Sakti* or energy of the god, otherwise called his wife. The origin of the system is not fully explained; nor is the date of its rise ascertained. The worship assumes wild, extravagant forms, generally obscene, sometimes bloody. It is divided into two schools—that of the right hand and that of the left. The former runs into mysticism and magic in compli-

Influence of the Tantras.

Worship of the Sakti.

[1] Raja Narayan Basu (Bose), in enumerating the sacred books of Hinduism, excluded the philosophical systems and included the Tantras. He was and, we believe, is a leading man in the Adi Brahma Somaj.

cated observances, and the latter into the most appalling licentiousness. The worship of the Sakti, or female principle, has become a most elaborate system. The beings adored are "the most outrageous divinities which man has ever conceived."[1] Sorcery began early in India; but it is in connection with this system that it attains to full development. Human sacrifices are a normal part of the worship when fully performed. We cannot go farther into detail. It is profoundly saddening to think that such abominations are committed; it is still more saddening to think that they are performed as a part of divine worship. Conscience, however, is so far alive that these detestable rites are practiced only in secret, and few, if any, are willing to confess that they have been initiated as worshipers.

Modern ritual.

We have not yet said much about the ritual of modern days. It is exceedingly complicated. In the case of the god Siva the rites are as follows, when performed by a priest in the temple:

Worship of Siva.

The Brahman first bathes, then enters the temple and bows to the god. He anoints the image with clarified butter or boiled oil; pours pure water over it; and then wipes it dry. He grinds some white powder, mixing it with water; dips

[1] Barth, as above, p. 202.

the ends of his three forefingers in it and draws them across the image. He sits down; meditates; places rice and *durva* grass on the image—places a flower on his own head, and then on the top of the image; then another flower on the image, and another, and another—accompanying each act with the recitation of sacred spells; places white powder, flowers, bilva-leaves, incense, meat-offerings, rice, plantains, and a lamp before the image; repeats the name of Siva, with praises, then prostrates himself before the image. In the evening he returns, washes his feet, prostrates himself before the door, opens the door, places a lamp within, offers milk, sweet-meats, and fruits to the image, prostrates himself before it, locks the door, and departs.

Very similar is the worship paid to Vishnu:

Worship of Vishnu.

The priest bathes, and then awakes the sleeping god by blowing a shell and ringing a bell. More abundant offerings are made than to Siva. About noon, fruits, roots, soaked peas, sweet-meats, etc., are presented. Then, later, boiled rice, fried herbs, and spices; but no flesh, fish, nor fowl. After dinner, betel-nut. The god is then left to sleep, and the temple is shut up for some hours. Toward evening curds, butter, sweet-meats, fruits, are presented. At sunset a lamp is brought, and fresh offerings made. Lights are waved before the image; a small bell is rung; water is presented for washing the mouth, face, and feet, with a towel to dry them. In a few minutes the offerings and the lamp are removed; and the god is left to sleep in the dark.

The prescribed worship is not always fully performed. Still, sixteen things are essential, of which the following are the most important:

"Preparing a seat for the god; invoking his presence; bathing the image; clothing it; putting the string round it; offering perfumes; flowers; incense; lamps; offerings of fruits and prepared eatables: betel-nut; prayers; circumambulation. An ordinary worshiper presents some of the offerings, mutters a short prayer or two, when circumambulating the image, the rest being done by the priest."[1]

We give one additional specimen of the ritual:

"As an atonement for unwarily eating or drinking what is forbidden eight hundred repetitions of the Gayatri prayer should be preceded by three suppressions of the breath, water being touched during the recital of the following text: 'The bull roars; he has four horns, three feet, two heads, seven hands, and is bound by a threefold cord; he is the mighty, resplendent being, and pervades mortal men.'"[2]

The bull is understood to be justice personified. All Brahmanical ceremonies exhibit, we may say, ritualism and symbolism run mad.

Caste.

The most prominent and characteristic institution of Hinduism is caste. The power of caste is as irrational as it is unbounded; and it works almost unmixed evil. The touch—even the shadow—of a low caste man pollutes. The scriptural precept, "Honor all men," appears to a true Hindu infinitely absurd. He honors and worships a cow; but he shrinks with horror from the touch of a Mhar or Mang. Even Brahmans, if they come from different provinces, will not eat together. Thus Hinduism separates man from man; it goes on dividing and

[1] So writes Vans Kennedy, a good authority. The rites, however, vary with varying places.

[2] *Asiatic Researches*, v, p. 356.

still dividing; and new fences to guard imaginary purity are continually added.

Treatment of women.

The whole treatment of women has gradually become most tyrannical and unjust. In very ancient days they were held in considerable respect; but, for ages past, the idea of woman has been steadily sinking lower and lower, and her rights have been more and more assailed. The burning of widows has been prohibited by enactment; but the awful rite would in many places be restored were it not for the strong hand of the British government. The practice of marrying women in childhood is still generally—all but universally—prevalent; and when, owing to the zeal of reformers, a case of widow-marriage occurs, its rarity makes it be hailed as a signal triumph. Multitudes of the so-called widows were never really wives, their husbands (so-called) having died in childhood. Widows are subjected to treatment which they deem worse than death; and yet their number, it is calculated, amounts to about twenty-one millions! More cruel and demoralizing customs than exist in India in regard to women can hardly be found among the lowest barbarians. We are glad to escape from dwelling on points so exceedingly painful.

Widows.

IV.

CONTRAST WITH CHRISTIANITY.

THE immense difference between the Hindu and Christian religions has doubtless already frequently suggested itself to the reader. It will not be necessary, therefore, to dwell on this topic at very great length. The contrast forces itself upon us at every point.

The Aryas and Israelites—their probable future, about 1500 B.C.

When, about fifteen centuries B. C., the Aryas were victoriously occupying the Panjab, and the Israelites were escaping from the "iron furnace" of Egypt, if one had been asked which of the two races would probably rise to the highest conception of the divine, and contribute most largely to the well-being of mankind, the answer, quite possibly, might have been, the Aryas. Egypt, with its brutish idolatries, had corrupted the faith of the Israelites, and slavery had crushed all manliness out of them. Yet how wonderful has been their after-history! Among ancient religions that of the Old Testament stands absolutely

Contrast of their after-history.

unique, and in the fullness of time it blossomed into Christianity. How is the marvel to be explained? We cannot account for it except by ascribing it to a divine election of the Israelites and a providential training intended to fit them to become the teachers of the world. "Salvation is of the Jews."

The contrast between the teachings of the Bible and those of the Hindu books is simply infinite.

Hindu theology compared with Christian.

The conception of a purely immaterial Being, infinite, eternal, and unchangeable, which is that of the Bible regarding God, is entirely foreign to the Hindu books. Their doctrine is various, but, in every case, erroneous. It is absolute pantheism, or polytheism, or an inconsistent blending of polytheism and pantheism, or atheism.

Equally striking is the contrast between Christianity and Hinduism as to the attributes of God. According to the former, he is omnipresent; omnipotent; possessed of every excellence—holiness, justice, goodness, truth. According to the chief Hindu philosophy, the Supreme is devoid of attributes—devoid of consciousness. According to the popular conception, when the Supreme becomes conscious he is developed into three gods, who possess respectively the qualities of truth, passion, and darkness.

Conception of God.

"God is a Spirit." "God is light." "God is love." These sublime declarations have no counterparts in Hindustan.

He is "the Father of spirits," according to the Bible. According to Hinduism, the individual spirit is a portion of the divine. Even the common people firmly believe this.

Every thing is referred by Hinduism to God as its immediate cause. A Christian is continually shocked by the Hindus ascribing all sin to God as its source.

The object of worship.

The adoration of God as a Being possessed of every glorious excellence is earnestly commanded in the Bible. "Thou shalt worship the Lord thy God; and him only shalt thou serve." In India the Supreme is never worshiped; but any one of the multitudinous gods may be so; and, in fact, every thing can be worshiped *except* God. A maxim in the mouth of every Hindu is the following: "Where there is faith, there is God." Believe the stone a god and it is so.

The sense of sin.

Every sin being traced to God as its ultimate source, the sense of personal guilt is very slight among Hindus. Where it exists it is generally connected with ceremonial defilement or the breach of some one of the innumerable and meaningless rites of the religion. How unlike in all this is the Gospel! The Bible dwells with all possible earnestness on the evil of sin, not of ceremonial but moral defilement—the transgression of the divine law, the eternal law of right.

Atonement.

How important a place in the Christian system is held by atonement, the great atonement made by Christ, it is unnecessary to say. Nor need we enlarge on the extraordinary power it exercises over the human heart, at once filling it with contrition, hatred of sin, and overflowing joy. We turn to Hinduism. Alas! we find that the earnest questionings and higher views of the ancient thinkers have in a great degree been ignored in later times. Sacrifice in its original form has passed away. Atonement is often spoken of; but it is only some paltry device or other, such as eating the five products of the cow, going on pilgrimage to some sacred shrine, paying money to the priests, or, it may be, some form of bodily penance. Such expedients leave no impression on the heart as to the true nature and essential evil of sin.

Salvation.

Salvation, in the Christian system, denotes deliverance, not only from the punishment of sin, but from its power, implying a renovation of the moral nature. The entire man is to be rectified in heart, speech, and behavior. The perfection of the individual, and, through that, the perfection of society, are the objects aimed at; and the consummation desired is the doing of the will of God on earth as it is done in heaven. Now, of all this, surely a magnificent ideal, we find in Hinduism no trace whatever.

Sanctification.

Christianity is emphatically a religion of hope; Hinduism may be designated a religion of despair. The trials of life are many and great. Christianity bids us regard them as discipline from a Father's hand, and tells us that affliction rightly borne yields "the peaceable fruits of righteousness." To death the Christian looks forward without fear; to him it is a quiet sleep, and the resurrection draws nigh. Then comes the beatific vision of God. Glorified in soul and body, the companion of angels and saints, strong in immortal youth, he will serve without let or hinderance the God and Saviour whom he loves. To the Hindu the trials of life are penal, not remedial. At death his soul passes into another body. Rightly, every human soul animates in succession eighty-four lacs (8,400,000) of bodies—the body of a human being, or a beast, or a bird, or a fish, or a plant,

Views of life.

or a stone, according to desert. This weary, all but endless, round of births fills the mind of a Hindu with the greatest horror. At last the soul is lost in God as a drop mingles with the ocean. Individual existence and consciousness then cease. The thought is profoundly sorrowful that this is the cheerless faith of countless multitudes. No wonder, though, the great tenet of Hinduism is this—*Existence is misery.*

The great tenet of Hinduism.

So much for the future of the individual. Regarding the future of the race Hinduism speaks in equally cheerless terms. Its golden age lies in the immeasurably distant past; and the further we recede from it the deeper must we plunge into sin and wretchedness. True, ages and ages hence the "age of truth" returns, but it returns only to pass away again and torment us with the memory of lost purity and joy. The experience of the universe is thus an eternal renovation of hope and disappointment. In the struggle between good and evil there is no final triumph for the good. We tread a fated, eternal round from which there is no escape; and alike the hero fights and the martyr dies in vain.

The future of the race.

The struggle between good and evil.

It is remarkable that acute intellectual men, as

many of the Hindu poets were, should never have grappled with the problem of the divine government of the world.

The future of the Aryan race.

Equally notable is the unconcern of the Veda as to the welfare and the future of even the Aryan race. But how sublime is the promise given to Abraham that in him and his seed all nations of the earth should be blessed! Renan has pointed with admiration to the confidence entertained at all times by the Jew in a brilliant and happy future for mankind. The ancient Hindu cared not about the future of his neighbors, and doubtless even the expression "human race" would have been unintelligible to him. Nor is there any pathos in the Veda. There is no deep sense of the sorrows of life. Max Müller has affixed the epithet "transcendent" to the Hindu mind. Its bent was much more toward the metaphysical, the mystical, the incomprehensible than toward the moral and the practical. Hence endless subtleties, more meaningless and unprofitable than ever occupied the mind of Talmudist or schoolman of the Middle Ages.

The words of St. Paul illustrated by Hinduism.

But finally, on this part of the subject, the development of Indian religion supplies a striking comment on the words of St. Paul:

"The invisible things of God are clearly seen, being understood from the things that are made. But when they knew God they glorified him not as God, neither were thankful, but became vain in their imaginations, and their foolish heart was darkened."

Moral power.

Hinduism is deplorably deficient in power to raise and purify the human soul, from having no high example of moral excellence. Its renowned sages were noted for irritability and selfishness—great men at cursing; and the gods for the most part were worse. Need we say how gloriously rich the Gospel is in having in the character of Christ the realized ideal of every possible excellence?

Ethical effect of Hinduism.

Summa religionis est imitari quem colis: "It is the sum of religion to imitate the being worshiped;"[1] or, as the Hindus express it: "As is the deity such is the devotee." Worship the God revealed in the Bible, and you become godlike. The soul strives, with divine aid, to "purify itself even as God is pure." But apply the principle to Hinduism. Alas! the Pantheon is almost a pandemonium. Krishna, who in these days is the chief deity to at least a hundred millions of people, does not possess one elevated attribute. If, in the circumstances, society does not become a moral pesthouse it

[1] Cicero.

is only because the people continue better than their religion. The human heart, though fallen, is not fiendish. It has still its purer instincts; and, when the legends about abominable gods and goddesses are falling like mildew, these are still to some extent kept alive by the sweet influences of earth and sky and by the charities of family life. When the heart of woman is about to be swept into the abyss her infant's smile restores her to her better self. Thus family life does not go to ruin; and so long as that anchor holds society will not drift on the rocks that stand so perilously near. Still, the state of things is deplorably distressing.

The people better than their religion.

The doctrine of the incarnation is of fundamental importance in Christianity. It seems almost profanation to compare it with the Hindu teaching regarding the Avataras, or descents of Vishnu. It is difficult to extract any meaning out of the three first manifestations, when the god became in succession a fish, a boar, and a tortoise. Of the great "descents" in Rama and Krishna we have already spoken. The ninth Avatara was that of Buddha, in which the deity descended for the purpose of deceiving men, making them deny the gods, and leading them to destruction. So blasphemous an idea

The doctrine of incarnation.

may seem hardly possible, even for the bewildered mind of India; but this is doubtless the Brahmanical explanation of the rise and progress of Buddhism. It was fatal error, but inculcated by a divine being. Even the sickening tales of Krishna and his amours are less shocking than this. When we turn from such representations of divinity to "the Word made flesh" we seem to have escaped from the pestilential air of a charnel-house to the sweet, pure breath of heaven.

V.

HINDUISM IN CONTACT WITH CHRISTIANITY.

We have used the word *reformer* in this Tract. We formerly noted that, in India, there have arisen from time to time men who saw and sorrowed over the erroneous doctrines and degrading rites of the popular system.

Attempted reforms.

In quite recent times they have had successors. Some account of their work may form a fitting conclusion to our discussion.

With the large influx into India of Christian ideas it was to be expected that some impression would be made on Hinduism. We do not refer to conversion—the full acceptance of the Christian faith. Christianity has advanced and is advancing in India more rapidly than is generally supposed; but far beyond the circle of those who "come out and are separate" its mighty power is telling on Hinduism. The great fundamental truths of the Gospel, when once uttered and understood, can hardly be forgotten. Disliked and denied

Advance of Christianity in India.

they may be; but forgotten? No. Thus they gradually win their way, and multitudes who have no thought of becoming Christians are ready to admit that they are beautiful and true; for belief and practice are often widely separated in Hindu minds.

But it was to be expected that the new ideas pouring into India—and among these we include not only distinctively Christian ideas, but Western thought generally—would manifest their presence and activity in concrete forms, in attempted reconstructions of religion. The most remarkable example of such a reconstruction is exhibited in the Brahmo Somaj (more correctly Brahma Samaj)—which may be rendered the "Church of God."

The Brahma Samaj.

It is traceable to the efforts of a truly distinguished man, Rammohun Roy. He was a person of studious habits, intelligent, acute, and deeply in earnest on the subject of religion. He studied not only Hinduism in its various forms, but Buddhism, Mohammedanism, and Christianity. He was naturally an eclectic, gathering truth from all quarters where he thought he could find it. A specially deep impression was made on his mind by Christianity; and in 1820 he published a book with

Rammohun Roy.

the remarkable title, *The Precepts of Jesus the Guide to Peace and Happiness.* Very frequently he gave expression to the sentiment that the teachings of Christ were the truest and deepest that he knew. Still, he did not believe in Christ's divinity.

Effect of Christianity upon him.

In January, 1830, a place of worship was opened by Rammohun Roy and his friends. It was intended for the worship of one God, without idolatrous rites of any kind. This was undoubtedly a very important event, and great was the interest aroused in connection with it. Rammohun Roy, however, visited Britain in 1831, and died at Bristol in 1833; and the cause for which he had so earnestly labored in India languished for a time. But in the year 1841 Debendernath Tagore, a man of character and wealth, joined the Brahmo Somaj, and gave a kind of constitution to it. It was fully organized by 1844. No definite declaration, however, had been made as to the authority of the Vedas; but, after a lengthened period of inquiry and discussion, a majority of the Somaj rejected the doctrine of their infallibility by 1850. "The rock of intuition" now began to be spoken of; man's reason was his sufficient guide. Still, great respect was cher-

Debendernath Tagore.

ished for the ancient belief and customs of the land. But in 1858 a new champion appeared on the scene, in the well-known Keshub Chunder Sen. Ardent, impetuous, ambitious—full of ideas derived from Christian sources[1]—he could not brook the slow movements of the Somaj in the path of reform. Important changes, both religious and social, were pressed by him; and the more conservative Debendernath somewhat reluctantly consented to their introduction. Matters were, however, brought to a crisis by the marriage of two persons of different castes in 1864. In February, 1865, the progressive party formally severed their connection with the original Somaj; and in August, 1869, they opened a new place of worship of their own. Since this time the original or Adi Somaj has been little heard of, and its movement—if it has moved at all—has been retrogressive. The new Somaj—the Brahmo Somaj of India, as it called itself—under the guidance of Mr. Sen became very active. A missionary institute was set up, and preachers were sent over a great part of India. Much was accomplished on behalf of women; and in 1872

Keshub Chunder Sen.

Formation of a new Samaj.

[1] We learned from his own lips that among the books which most deeply impressed him were the Bible and the writings of Dr. Chalmers.

a Marriage Act for members of the Somaj was passed by the Indian legislature, which legalized union between people of different castes, and fixed on fourteen as the lowest age for the marriage of females. These were important reforms.

Mr. Sen's influence was naturally and necessarily great; but in opposing the venerable leader of the original Somaj he had set an example which others were quite willing to copy.

Discontent growing.

Several of his followers began to demand more radical reforms than he was willing to grant. The autocracy exercised by Mr. Sen was strongly objected to, and a constitution of the Somaj was demanded. Mr. Sen openly maintained that heaven from time to time raises up men endowed with special powers, and commissioned to introduce new forms or "dispensations" of religion; and his conduct fully proved that he regarded himself as far above his followers. Complaints became louder; and although the eloquence and genius of Keshub were able to keep the rebellious elements from exploding it was evident, as early as 1873, that a crisis was approaching. This came in 1878, when Mr. Sen's daughter was married to the Maharaja of Kuch Behar. The bride was not fourteen, and the bridegroom was sixteen. Now, Mr. Sen had been earnest and successful in getting the Brahmo Marriage Act passed, which ruled that the lowest marriageable age for a woman was fourteen, and for a man eighteen. Here was gross inconsistency. What could explain it? "Ambition," exclaimed great numbers; "the wish to exalt himself and his daughter by alliance with a prince." But Mr. Sen declared that he had consented to the marriage in consequence of an express intimation that such was the will of heaven. Mr. Sen denied miracles, but believed in inspiration; and of his own inspiration he seems to have entertained no doubt. We thus obtain a glimpse into the peculiar working of his mind. Every full conviction, every strong wish of his own he ascribed to divine suggestion. This put him in a position of extreme peril. It was clear that an enthusiastic, imaginative, self-reliant nature like his might thus be borne on to any extent of fanaticism.

Revolt; a third Samaj.

A great revolt from Mr. Sen's authority now took place, and the Sadharan Samaj was organized in May, 1878. An appeal had been made to the members generally, and no fewer than twenty-one provincial Samajes, with more than four hundred members, male and female, joined the new society. This number amounted to about two thirds of the whole body. Keshub and his friends denounced the rebels in very bitter language; and yet, in one point of view, their secession was a relief. Men of abilities equal, and education superior, to his own had hitherto acted as a drag on his movements; he was now delivered from their interference and could deal with the admiring and submissive remnant as he pleased. Ideas that had been working in his mind now attained rapid development. Within two

"New Dispensation."

years the flag of the "New Dispensation" was raised; and of that dispensation Mr. Sen was the undoubted head. Very daring was the language Mr. Sen used in a public lecture regarding this new creation. He claimed equality for it with the Jewish and Christian dispensations, and for himself "singular" authority and a divine commission.

Its creed.

In the Creed of the New Dispensation the name of Christ does not occur. The articles were as follows:

a. One God, one Scripture, one Church. *b.* Eternal progress of the soul. *c.* Communion of prophets and saints. *d.* Fatherhood and motherhood of God. *e.* Brotherhood of man and sisterhood of woman.

f. Harmony of knowledge and holiness, love and work, yoga and asceticism in their highest development. *g.* Loyalty to sovereign.

Omission of Christ's name.

The omission of Christ's name is the more remarkable because Mr. Sen spoke much of him in his public lectures. He had said in May, 1879, "None but Jesus, none but Jesus, none but Jesus ever deserved this precious diadem, India; and Jesus shall have it." But he clearly indicated that the Christ he sought was an Indian Christ; one who was "a Hindu in faith," and who would help the Hindus to "realize their national idea of a yogi" (ascetic).

"Motherhood of God."

Let it be noted that, from the beginning of his career, Mr. Sen had spoken earnestly of the fatherhood of God and the brotherhood of man—though these great conceptions are not of Hindu origin. It is difficult to see why, in later days, he insisted so much on the "motherhood of God." Perhaps it was a repetition—he probably would have called it an exaltation—of the old Hindu idea, prevalent especially among the worshipers of Siva, that there is a female counterpart—a Sakti—of every divinity. Or, possibly, it may have been to conciliate the worshipers of Durga and Kali, those great goddesses of Bengal.

Public proclamation said to be from God.

A public proclamation was soon issued, purporting to be from God himself, as India's mother. The whole thing was very startling; many, even of Keshub's friends, declared it blasphemous. Next, in the "Flag Ceremony," the flag or banner of the New Dispensation received a homage scarcely distinguishable from worship. Then—as if in strict imitation of the ancient adoration of Agni, or Fire—a pile of wood was lighted, clarified butter poured on it, and prayers addressed to it, ending thus—"O, brilliant Fire! in thee we behold our resplendent Lord." This was, at least, symbolism run wild; and every one, except those who were prepared to follow their leader to all lengths, saw that in a land like India, wedded to idolatry, it was fearfully perilous.

"Apostolic Durbar."

In March, 1881, Mr. Sen and his friends introduced celebrations which, to Christian minds, seemed a distressing caricature of the Christian sacraments. Other institutions followed; an Apostolic Durbar (Court of Apostles), for instance, was established. There was no end to Mr. Sen's inventiveness.

In a public lecture delivered in January, 1883, on "Asia's message to Europe," he elaborately expounded the idea that all the great religions are of Asiatic origin, and that all of them are true, and that the one thing required to constitute the faith of the future—the religion of humanity—is the blending of all these varied Oriental systems into one.

Inconsistencies between Mr. Sen's public and private utterances.

It was not easy to reconcile Mr. Sen's public utterances with his private ones—though far be it from us to tax him with insincerity. Thus, in an interview extending over two hours, which the writer and two missionary friends had with him a week or so before the lecture now referred to, he said he accepted as true and vital all the leading doctrines of the Christian faith, with the exception of the resurrection of Christ. But another fundamental difference remained—he avowedly dissented from the orthodox creed in rejecting the miraculous element in Scripture. At an interview I had with him some time before he earnestly disclaimed all intention to put Christ on a level with Buddha or Mohammed. "I am educating my friends," he said, "to understand and approve of Christianity; I have not yet said my last word about Christ." It is a solemn question, Had he said it when his career was ended? If so, it was far from a satisfactory word.

Mr. Sen's policy of reserve.

His policy of reserve and adaptation had probably kept him from uttering all that was in his heart; but it was a sorely mistaken policy. Had he temporized less he would have accomplished more.

Since the death of Mr. Sen there has been a violent dispute between his family and the "Apostolic Durbar," on one side, and one of his ablest followers, on the other; and the New Dispensation will probably split in two, if it does not perish altogether.

The Sadharan Samaj.

In the meantime, the Sadharan Samaj, which broke off from Keshub's party in 1878, has been going on with no small vigor. Vagaries, either in doctrine or rites, have been carefully shunned; its partisans profess a pure Theistic creed and labor diligently in the cause of social reform. Their position is nearly that of Unitarian Christianity, and we fear they are not at present approximating to the full belief of the Church Catholic.

Movements in western India.

Tenets of the Prarthana Sabha.

Very similar in character to the Brahmo Somaj is the Prarthana Somaj in western India. As far back as 1850, or a little earlier, there was formed a society called the Prarthana Sabha (Prayer-meeting). Its leading tenets were as follows:

1. I believe in one God. 2. I renounce idol-worship. 3. I will do my best to lead a moral life. 4. If I commit any sin through the weakness of my moral nature I will repent of it and ask the pardon of God.

The society, after some time, began to languish; but in 1867 it was revived under the name of Prarthana Somaj. Its chief branches are in Bombay, Poona, Ahmedabad, and Surat.

An interesting movement called the Arya Samaj was commenced a few years ago by a Pandit—Dayanand Sarasvati. He received the Vedas as fully inspired, but maintained that they taught monotheism—Agni, Indra, and all the rest being merely different names of God. It was a desperate effort to save the reputation of the ancient books; but, as all Sanskrit scholars saw at a glance, the whole idea was a delusion. The Pandit is now dead; and the Arya Samaj may not long survive him.

Arya Samaj.

At the time we write we hear of an attempt to defend idolatry and caste made by men of considerable education.

The so-called "Theosophists" have, for several years, been active in India. Of existing religions, Buddhism is their natural ally. They are atheists. A combination which they formed with the Arya Samaj speedily came to an end.

Theosophists.

Lastly, the followers of Mr. Bradlaugh are diligent in supplying their books to Indian students.

Poor India! No wonder if her mind is bewildered as she listens to such a Babel of voices. The state of things in India now strikingly resembles that which existed in the Roman Empire at the rise of Christianity; when East and West were brought into the closest contact, and a great conflict of systems of thought took place in consequence.

But even as one hostile form of gnostic belief rose after another, and rose only to fall—and as the greatest and best-disciplined foe of early Christianity—the later Platonism—gave way before the steady, irreristible march of gospel truth, so—we have every reason to hope—it will be yet again. The Christian feels his heart swell in his breast as he thinks what, in all human probability, India will be a century, or even half a century, hence. O what a new life to that fairest of Eastern lands when she casts herself in sorrow and supplication at the feet of the living God, and then rises to proclaim to a listening world

"Her deep repentance and her new-found joy!"

May God hasten the advent of that happy day!

THE RISE AND DECLINE OF ISLAM.

OUTLINE OF THE ESSAY.

THE progress of Islam was slow until Mohammed cast aside the precepts of toleration and adopted an aggressive, militant policy. Then it became rapid. The motives which animated the armies of Islam were mixed—material and spiritual. Without the truths contained in the system success would have been impossible, but neither without the sword would the religion have been planted in Arabia, nor beyond. The alternatives offered to conquered peoples were Islam, the sword, or tribute. The drawbacks and attractions of the system are examined. The former were not such as to deter men of the world from embracing the faith. The sexual indulgences sanctioned by it are such as to make Islam "the Easy way."

The spread of Islam was stayed whenever military success was checked. The Faith was meant for Arabia and not for the world, hence it is constitutionally incapable of change or development. The degradation of woman hinders the growth of freedom and civilization under it.

Christianity is contrasted in the means used for its propagation, the methods it employed in grappling with and overcoming the evils that it found existing in the world, in the relations it established between the sexes, in its teaching with regard to the respective duties of the civil and spiritual powers, and, above all, in its redeeming character, and then the conclusion come to that Christianity is divine in its origin.

THE RISE AND DECLINE OF ISLAM.

INTRODUCTION.

Islam pre-eminent in its rapid spread.

AMONG the religions of the earth Islam must take the precedence in the rapidity and force with which it spread. Within a very short time from its planting in Arabia the new faith had subdued great and populous provinces. In half a dozen years, counting from the death of the founder, the religion prevailed throughout Arabia, Syria, Persia, and Egypt, and before the close of the century it ruled supreme over the greater part of the vast populations from Gibraltar to the Oxus, from the Black Sea to the river Indus.

Propagation far quicker than of Christianity.

In comparison with this grand outburst the first efforts of Christianity were, to the outward eye, faint and feeble, and its extension so gradual that what the Mohammedan religion achieved in ten or twenty years it took the faith of Jesus long centuries to accomplish.

Object of the Tract.

The object of these few pages is, *first*, to inquire briefly into the causes which led to the marvelous rapidity of the first movement of Islam: *secondly*, to consider the reasons which eventually stayed its advance; and, *lastly*, to ascertain why Mohammedan countries have kept so far in the rear of other lands in respect of intellectual and social progress. In short, the question is how it was that, Pallas-like, the faith sprang ready-armed from the ground, conquering and to conquer, and why, the weapons dropping from its grasp, Islam began to lose its pristine vigor, and finally relapsed into inactivity.

I.

THE RAPID SPREAD OF ISLAM.

Two periods in the mission of Mohammed.

THE personal ministry of Mohammed divides itself into two distinct periods: first, his life at Mecca as a preacher and a prophet; second, his life at Medina as a prophet and a king.

I. Ministry at Mecca, A. D. 609-622.

It is only in the first of these periods that Islam at all runs parallel with Christianity. The great body of his fellow-citizens rejected the ministry of Mohammed and bitterly opposed his claims. His efforts at Mecca were, therefore, confined to teaching and preaching and to the publishing of the earlier "Suras," or chapters of his "Revelation." After some thirteen years spent thus his converts, to the number of about a hundred and fifty men and women, were forced by the persecution of the Coreish (the ruling tribe at Mecca, from which Mohammed was descended) to quit their native city and emigrate to Medina.[1] A hundred more had previously fled from Mecca for

Success at Mecca limited.

[1] See *Life of Mohammed*, p. 138. Smith & Elder.

the same cause, and found refuge at the court of the Negus, or king of Abyssinia; and there was already a small company of followers among the citizens of Medina. At the utmost, therefore, the number of disciples gained over by the simple resort to teaching and preaching did not, during the first twelve years of Mohammed's ministry, exceed a few hundreds. It is true that the soil of Mecca was stubborn and (unlike that of Judea) wholly unprepared. The cause also, at times, became the object of sustained and violent opposition. Even so much of success was consequently, under the peculiar circumstances, remarkable. But it was by no means singular. The progress fell far short of that made by Christianity during the corresponding period of its existence,[1] and indeed by many reformers who have been the preachers of a new faith. It gave no promise whatever of the marvelous spectacle that was about to follow.

II. Change of policy at Medina, A. D. 622-632.

Having escaped from Mecca and found a new and congenial home in Medina, Mohammed was not long in changing his front. At Mecca, surrounded by enemies, he taught toleration. He was simply the preacher commissioned to deliver a message, and bidden to leave the respon-

[1] *Life of Mohammed*, p. 172, where the results are compared.

Arabia converted from Medina at the point of the sword.

sibility with his Master and his hearers. He might argue with the disputants, but it must be "in a way most mild and gracious;" for "in religion" (such was his teaching before he reached Medina) "there should be neither violence nor constraint."[1] At Medina the precepts of toleration were quickly cast aside and his whole policy reversed. No sooner did Mohammed begin to be recognized and obeyed as the chief of Medina than he proceeded to attack the Jewish tribes settled in the neighborhood because they refused to acknowledge his claims and believe in him as a prophet foretold in their Scriptures; two of these tribes were exiled, and the third exterminated in cold blood. A. D. 623. In the second year after the Hegira, or flight from Mecca (the period from which the Mohammedan era dates), he began to plunder the caravans of the Coreish, which passed near to Medina on their mercantile journeys between Arabia and Syria. So popular did the cause of the now militant and marauding prophet speedily become among the citizens of Medina and the tribes around A. D. 630. that, after many battles fought with varying success, he was able, in the eighth year of the

[1] *Life of Mohammed*, p. 341; Sura ii, 257; xxix, 46.

Hegira to re-enter his native city at the head of ten thousand armed followers. Thenceforward success was assured. None dared to oppose his pretensions. And before his death, in the eleventh year of the Hegira, all Arabia, from Bab-el-Mandeb and Oman to the confines of the Syrian desert, was forced to submit to the supreme authority of the now kingly prophet and to recognize the faith and obligations of Islam.[1]

A. D. 632.

This *Islam*, so called from its demanding the entire "surrender" of the believer to the will and service of God, is based on the recognition of Mohammed as a prophet foretold in the Jewish and Christian Scriptures—the last and greatest of the prophets. On him descended the Koran from time to time, an immediate revelation from the Almighty. Idolatry and polytheism are with iconoclastic zeal denounced as sins of the deepest dye; while the unity of the Deity is proclaimed as the grand and cardinal doctrine of the faith. Divine

Religion of Mohammed described.

[1] The only exceptions were the Jews of Kheibar and the Christians of Najran, who were permitted to continue in the profession of their faith. They were, however, forced by Omar to quit the peninsula, which thenceforward remained exclusively Mohammedan.

"Islam" is a synonym for the Mussulman faith. Its original meaning is "surrender" of one's self to God.

providence pervades the minutest concerns of life, and predestination is taught in its most naked form. Yet prayer is enjoined as both meritorious and effective; and at five stated times every day must it be specially performed. The duties generally of the moral law are enforced, though an evil laxity is given in the matter of polygamy and divorce. Tithes are demanded as alms for the poor. A fast during the month of Ramzan must be kept throughout the whole of every day; and the yearly pilgrimage to Mecca—an ancient institution, the rites of which were now divested of their heathenish accompaniments—maintained. The existence of angels and devils is taught, and heaven and hell are depicted in material colors—the one of sensuous pleasure, the other of bodily torment. Finally, the resurrection, judgment, and retribution of good and evil are set forth in great detail. Such was the creed —"*There is no god but the* LORD, *and* MOHAMMED *is his prophet*"—to which Arabia now became obedient.

Arabia apostatizes; but is speedily reconquered and reclaimed, A. D. 633.

But immediately on the death of Mohammed the entire peninsula relapsed into apostasy. Medina and Mecca remained faithful; but every-where else the land seethed with rebellion. Some tribes joined the "false prophets," of whom four had arisen in different parts of Arabia; some relapsed into their ancient heathenism; while others proposed a compromise—they would observe the stated times of prayer, but would be excused the tithe. Every-where was rampant anarchy. The apostate tribes attacked Medina, but were repulsed by the brave old Caliph Abu Bekr, who refused to abate one jot or tittle, as the successor of Mohammed, of the obligations of Islam. Eleven columns were sent forth under as many leaders, trained in the warlike school of Mohammed. These fought their way, step by step, successfully; and thus, mainly through the wisdom and firmness of Abu Bekr and the valor and genius of Khalid, "the Sword of God," the Arab tribes, one by one, were overcome and forced back into their allegiance and the profession of Islam. The reconquest of Arabia and reimposition of Mohammedanism as the national faith, which it took a whole year to accomplish, is thus described by an Arabian author, who wrote at the close of the second century of the Mohammedan era:

After his decease there remained not one of the followers of the prophet that did not apostatize, saving only a small company of his "Companions" and kinsfolk, who hoped thus to secure the government to themselves. Hereupon Abu Bekr displayed marvelous skill, energy, and address, so that the power passed into his hands. . . . And thus he persevered until the apostate tribes were all brought back to their allegiance, some by kindly treatment, persuasion, and craft; some through terror and fear of the sword; and others by the prospect of power and wealth as well as by the lusts and pleasures of this life. And so it came to pass that all the Bedouin tribes were in the end converted outwardly, but not from inward conviction.[1]

The Arabs thus reclaimed were, at the first, sullen.

The temper of the tribes thus reclaimed by force of arms was at the first strained and sullen. But the scene soon changed. Suddenly the whole peninsula was shaken, and the people, seized with a burning zeal, issued forth to plant the new faith in other lands. It happened on this wise:

Roused by war-cry, they issue from the peninsula, A. D. 634, *et seq.*

The columns sent from Medina to reduce the rebellious tribes to the north-west on the Gulf of Ayla, and to the north-east on the Persian Gulf, came at once into collision with the Christian Bedouins of Syria on the one hand and with those of Mesopotamia on the other. These again were immediately supported by the neighboring forces of the Roman and Persian empires, whose vassals respectively they were. And so, before many months, Abu Bekr found his generals opposed by great and imposing armies on either side. He was,

The opposing forces.

[1] *Apology of Al Kindy, the Christian*, p. 18. Smith & Elder, 1882. This remarkable apologist will be noticed further below.

in fact, waging mortal combat at one and the same moment with the Kaiser and the Chosroes, the Byzantine emperor and the great king of Persia. The risk was imminent, and an appeal went forth for help to meet the danger. The battle-cry resounded from one end of Arabia to the other, and electrified the land. Levy after levy, *en masse*, started up at the call from every quarter of the peninsula, and the Bedouin tribes, as bees from their hive, streamed forth in swarms, animated by the prospect of conquest, plunder, and captive damsels, or, if slain in battle, by the still more coveted prize of the "martyr" in the material paradise of Mohammed. With a military ardor and new-born zeal in which carnal and spiritual aspirations were strangely blended, the Arabs rushed forth to the field, like the war-horse of Job, "that smelleth the battle afar off, the thunder of the captains and the shouting." Sullen constraint was in a moment transformed into an absolute devotion and fiery resolve to spread the faith. The Arab warrior became the missionary of Islam.

Arab enthusiasm.

It was now the care of Omar, the second caliph or ruler of the new-born empire, to establish a system whereby the spirit militant, called into existence with such force and fervor, might be rendered permanent. The entire Arabian people was subsidized. The surplus revenues which in rapidly increasing volume began to flow from the conquered lands into the Moslem treasuries were to the last farthing distributed among the soldiers of Arabian descent. The whole nation was enrolled, and the name of every warrior entered upon the roster of Islam. Forbidden to settle anywhere, and relieved from all other work, the Arab hordes became, in fact, a standing army threatening the world. Great bodies of armed men were kept thus ever mobilized, separate and in readiness for new enterprise.

Arabs, a military body, subsidized and mobilized by Omar.

The change which came over the policy of the Founder of the Faith at Medina, and paved the way for this marvelous system of world-wide rapine and conversion to Islam, is thus described by a thoughtful and sagacious writer:

Mission of Islam described by Fairbairn.

Medina was fatal to the higher capabilities of Islam. Mohammed became then a king; his religion was incorporated in a State that had to struggle for its life in the fashion familiar to the rough-handed sons of the desert. The prophet was turned into the legislator and commander; his revelations were now laws, and now military orders and manifestoes. The mission of Islam became one that only the sword could accomplish, robbery of the infidel became meritorious, and conquest the supreme duty it owed to the world. . . .

The religion which lived an unprospering and precarious life, so long as it depended on the prophetic word alone, became an aggressive and victorious power so soon as it was embodied in a State.[1]

And by Von Kremer.

Another learned and impartial authority tells us:

The Mussulman power under the first four caliphs was nothing but a grand religio-political association of Arab tribes for universal plunder and conquest under the holy banner of Islam, and the watchword, "There is no god but THE LORD, and Mohammed is his apostle." On pretext of spreading the only true religion the Arabs swallowed up fair provinces lying all around, and, driving a profitable business, enriched themselves simultaneously in a worldly sense.[2]

Religious merit of "fighting in the ways of the Lord."

The motives which nerved the armies of Islam were a strange combination of the lower instincts of nature with the higher aspirations of the spirit. To engage in the Holy War was the rarest and most blessed of all religious virtues, and conferred on the combatant a special merit; and side by side with it lay the bright prospect of spoil and female slaves, conquest and

[1] Principal Fairbairn: "The Primitive Polity of Islam," *Contemporary Review*, December, 1882, pp 866, 867

[2] Herr von Kremer, *Culturgeschichte des Orients*, unter den Chalifen, vol. i, p. 383.

glory. "Mount thy horse," said Osama ibn Zeid to Abu Bekr as he accompanied the Syrian army a little way on its march out of Medina. "Nay," replied the caliph, "I will not ride, but I will walk and soil my feet a little space in the ways of the Lord. Verily, every footstep in the ways of the Lord is equal in merit to manifold good works, and wipeth away a multitude of sins."[1] And of the "martyrs," those who fell in these crusading campaigns, Mohammed thus described the blessed state:

> Think not, in any wise, of those killed in the ways of the Lord, as if they were dead. Yea, they are alive, and are nourished with their Lord, exulting in that which God hath given them of his favor, and rejoicing in behalf of those who have not yet joined them, but are following after. No terror afflicteth them, neither are they grieved. —Sura iii.

Material fruits of Moslem crusade.

The material fruits of their victories raised the Arabs at once from being the needy inhabitants of a stony, sterile soil, where, with difficulty, they eked out a hardy subsistence, to be the masters of rich and luxuriant lands flowing with milk and honey. After one of his great victories on the plains of Chaldea, Khalid called together his troops, flushed with conquest, and lost in wonder at the exuberance around them, and thus

[1] *Annals of the Early Caliphate*, p. 9. Smith & Elder, 1883.

addressed them: "Ye see the riches of the land. Its paths drop fatness and plenty, so that the fruits of the earth are scattered abroad even as stones are in Arabia. If but as a provision for this present life, it were worth our while to fight for these fair fields and banish care and penury forever from us." Such were the aspirations dear to the heart of every Arab warrior. Again, after the battle of Jalola, a few years later, the treasure and spoil of the Persian monarch, captured by the victors, was valued at thirty million of dirhems (about a million sterling). The royal fifth (the crown share of the booty) was sent as usual to Medina under charge of Ziad, who, in the presence of the Caliph Omar, harangued the citizens in a glowing description of what had been won in Persia, fertile lands, rich cities, and endless spoil, besides captive maids and princesses.

In relating the capture of Medain (the ancient Ctesiphon) tradition revels in the untold wealth which fell into the hands of Sad, the conqueror, and his followers. Besides millions of treasure, there was endless store of gold and silver vessels, rich vestments, and rare and precious things.... The Arabs gazed bewildered at the tiara, brocaded vestments, jeweled armor, and splen-

Rich booty taken in the capital of Persia, A. D. 637.

did surroundings of the throne. They tell of a camel of silver, life-size, with a rider of gold, and of a golden horse with emeralds for teeth, the neck set with rubies, the trappings of gold. And we may read in Gibbon of the marvelous banqueting carpet, representing a garden, the ground of wrought gold, the walks of silver, the meadows of emeralds, rivulets of pearls, and flowers and fruits of diamonds, rubies, and rare gems. The precious metals lost their conventional value, gold was parted with for its weight in silver; and so on.[1]

Success in battle ascribed to divine aid.

It is the virtue of Islam that it recognizes a special providence, seeing the hand of God, as in every thing, so pre-eminently also in victory. When Sad, therefore, had established himself in the palace of the Chosroes he was not forgetful to render thanks in a service of praise. One of the princely mansions was turned for the moment into a temple, and there, followed by his troops, he ascribed the victory to the Lord of Hosts. The lesson accompanying the prayers was taken from a Sura (or chapter of the Koran) which speaks of Pharaoh and his riders being overwhelmed in the Red Sea,

[1] Gibbon's *Decline and Fall*, chapter li, and *Annals of the Early Caliphate*, p. 184.

and contains this passage, held to be peculiarly appropriate to the occasion:

> "How many gardens and fountains did they leave behind,
> And fields of corn, and fair dwelling-places,
> And pleasant things which they enjoyed!
> Even thus have WE made another people to inherit the same." [1]

"Martyrdom" in the field coveted by Moslem crusaders.

Such as fell in the conflict were called martyrs; a halo of glory surrounded them, and special joys awaited them even on the battle-field. And so it came to pass that the warriors of Islam had an unearthly longing for the crown of martyrdom. The Caliph Omar was inconsolable at the loss of his brother, Zeid, who fell in the fatal "Garden of Death," at the battle of Yemama: "Thou art returned home," he said to his son, Abdallah, "safe and sound, and Zeid is dead. Wherefore wast not thou slain before him? I wish not to see thy face." "Father," answered Abdallah, "he asked for the crown of martyrdom, and the Lord granted it. I strove after the same, but it was not given unto me." [2] It was the proud boast of the Saracens in their summons to the craven Greeks and Persians that "they loved death more than their foes loved life." Familiar with the

The Moslem crown of martyrdom.

[1] *Ibid.*; and Sura xliv, v. 25. *We*—that is, the Lord.

[2] *Annals of the Early Caliphate*, p. 46.

pictures drawn in the Koran of the beautiful "houries" of Paradise,[1] the Saracens believed that immediate fruition on the field of battle was the martyr's special prize. We are told of a Moslem soldier, fourscore years of age, who, seeing a comrade fall by his side, cried out, "O Paradise! how close art thou beneath the arrow's point and the falchion's flash! O Hashim! even now I see heaven opened, and black-eyed maidens all bridally attired, clasping thee in their fond embrace." And shouting thus the aged warrior, fired again with the ardor of youth, rushed upon the enemy and met the envied fate. For those who survived there was the less ethereal but closer prospect of Persian, Greek, or Coptic women, both maids and matrons, who, on "being taken captive by their right hand," were forthwith, according to the Koran, without stint of number, at the conqueror's will and pleasure. These, immediately they were made pris-

[1] See, for example, Sura lxxviii: "Verily for the pious there is a blissful abode: gardens and vineyards; and damsels with swelling bosoms, of a fitting age; and a full cup. Lovely large-eyed girls, like pearls hidden in their shells, a reward for that which the faithful shall have wrought. Verily We have created them of a rare creation, virgins, young and fascinating. . . . Modest damsels averting their eyes, whom no man shall have known before, nor any Jinn," etc.

The reader will not fail to be struck by the materialistic character of Mohammed's paradise.

oners, might (according to the example of Mohammed himself at Kheibar) be carried off without further ceremony to the victor's tent; and in this respect the Saracens certainly were nothing loath to execute upon the heathen the judgment written in their law. So strangely was religious fanaticism fed and fostered in the Moslem camp by incentives irresistible to the Arab—fight and foray, the spoil of war and captive charms.

Martial passages from Koran recited on field of battle.

The courage of the troops was stimulated by the divine promises of victory, which were read (and on like occasions still are read) at the head of each column drawn up for battle. Thus, on the field of Cadesiya, which decided the fate of Persia, the Sura *Jehad*, with the stirring tale of the thousand angels that fought on the Prophet's side at Bedr was recited, and such texts as these:

A. D. 635.

Stir up the faithful unto battle. If there be twenty steadfast among you they shall put two hundred to flight of the unbelievers, and a hundred shall put to flight a thousand. Victory is from the Lord. He is mighty and wise. I the Lord will cast terror into the hearts of the infidels. Strike off their heads and their fingers' ends. Beware lest ye turn your back in battle. Verily, he that turneth his back shall draw down upon himself the wrath of God. His abode shall be hell fire; an evil journey thither.

And we are told that on the recital of these verses "the heart of the people was refreshed and their eyes lightened, and they felt the tranquillity that ensueth thereupon." Three days they fought, and on the morning of the fourth, returning with unabated vigor to the charge, they scattered to the winds the vast host of Persia.[1]

Defeat of Byzantine army on the Yermuk, A. D. 634.

Nor was it otherwise in the great battle of the Yermuk, which laid Syria at the feet of the Arabs. The virgin vigor of the Saracens was fired by a wild fanatical zeal "to fight in the ways of the Lord," obtaining thus heavenly merit and a worldly prize—the spoil of Syria and its fair maidens ravished from their homes; or should they fall by the sword, the black-eyed houries waiting for them on the field of battle. "Of warriors nerved by this strange combination of earth and heaven, of the flesh and of the spirit, of the incentives at once of faith and rapine, of fanatical devotion to the prophet and deathless passion for the sex, ten might chase a hundred half-hearted Romans. The

[1] See Sura *Jehad*; also *Annals of the Early Caliphate*, p. 167, *et. seq*.

forty thousand Moslems were stronger far than the two hundred and forty thousand of the enemy." The combat lasted for weeks; but at the last the Byzantine force was utterly routed, and thousands hurled in wild confusion over the beetling cliffs of the Yermuk into the yawning chasm of Wacusa.[1]

Islam planted by aid of material force.

Such, then, was the nature of the Moslem propaganda, such the agency by which the faith was spread, and such the motives at once material and spiritual by which its martial missionaries were inspired. No wonder that the effete empires of Rome and Persia recoiled and quivered at the shock, and that province after province quickly fell under the sway of Islam. It is far from my intention to imply that the truths set forth by the new faith had nothing to do with its success. On the contrary, it may well be admitted that but for those truths success might have been impossible. The grand enunciation of the Divine Unity, and the duty of an absolute submission to the same; the recognition of a special providence reaching to the minutest details of life; the inculcation of prayer and other religious duties; the establishment of a code in which the leading principles of morality are enforced, and the acknowledgment of

[1] *Annals of the Early Caliphate*, p. 105, *et. seq.*

previous revelations in the Jewish and Christian Scriptures, told not only on the idolaters of Arabia and the fire-worshipers of Persia, but on Jews and Samaritans and the followers of a debased and priest-ridden Christianity. All this is true; but it is still not the less true that without the sword Islam would never have been planted even in Arabia, much less ever have spread to the countries beyond. The weapons of its warfare were "carnal," material, and earthly; and by them it conquered.

Alternatives offered to the conquered nations: Islam, the Sword, or Tribute.

The pressure brought to bear on the inhabitants of the countries overrun by Saracen arms was of the most stringent character. They were offered the triple alternative—ISLAM, the SWORD, or TRIBUTE. The first brought immediate relief. Acceptance of the faith not only stayed the enemy's hand, and conferred immunity from the perils of war, but associated the convert with his conquerors in the common brotherhood and in all the privileges of Islam.

Acceptance of Islam, immediate relief from the sword.

Reading the story of the spread of Islam, we are constantly told of this and that enemy, that "being beaten, he *believed* and embraced the faith." Take as an example of an every-day occurrence the story of Hormuzan.

A Persian prince of high rank long maintained a border warfare against the Moslems. At last he was taken prisoner and sent in chains to Medina. As he was conducted into the Great Mosque, Omar exclaimed, "Blessed be the Lord, that hath humbled this man and the like of him!" He bade them disrobe the prisoner and clothe him in sackcloth. Then, whip in hand, he upbraided him for his oft-repeated attacks and treachery. Hormuzan made as if fain to reply; then gasping, like one faint from thirst, he begged for water to drink. "Give it him," said the caliph, "and let him drink in peace." "Nay," cried the wretched captive, trembling, "I fear to drink, lest some one slay me unawares." "Thy life is safe," said Omar, "until thou hast drunk the water up." The words were no sooner said than Hormuzan emptied the vessel on the ground. "I wanted not the water," he said, "but quarter, and thou hast given it me." "Liar!" cried Omar, angrily, "thy life is forfeit." "But not," interposed the by-standers, "until he drink the water up." "Strange," said Omar, "the fellow hath deceived me; and yet I cannot spare the life of one who hath slain so many noble Moslems. I swear that thou shalt not gain by thy deceit unless thou wilt forthwith embrace Islam."

Upon that, "*believing*, he made profession of the true faith upon the spot;" and thenceforth, residing at Medina, he received a pension of the highest grade.[1]

Tribute and humiliation.

On the other hand, for those who held to their ancestral faith there was no escape from the second or the third alternative. If they would avoid the sword, or, having wielded it, were beaten, they must become tributary. Moreover, the payment of tribute is not the only condition enjoined by the Koran. "Fight against them (the Jews and Christians) until they pay tribute with the hand, *and are humbled*."[2] The command fell on willing ears. An ample interpretation was given to it. And so it came to pass that, though Jews and Christians were, on the payment of tribute, tolerated in the profession of their ancestral faith, they were yet subjected (and still are subjected) to severe humiliation.

Disabilities imposed on Jews and Christians.

The nature and extent of the degradation to which they were brought down, and the strength of the inducement to purchase exemption and the equality of civil rights, by surrendering their religion, may be learned from the provisions which were embodied in the code named *The Ordinance of Omar*, which has been more or less enforced from the earliest

[1] See *Annals*, etc., p. 253.

[2] Sura ix, v. 30.

times. Besides the tribute and various other imposts levied from the "People of the Book,"[1] and the duty of receiving Moslem travelers quartered upon them, the dress of both sexes must be distinguished by broad stripes of yellow. They are forbidden to appear on horseback, and if mounted on a mule or ass their stirrups must be of wood, and their saddles known by knobs of the same material. Their graves must not rise above the level of the soil, and the devil's mark is placed upon the lintel of their doors. Their children must be taught by Moslem masters, and the race, however able or well qualified, proscribed from any office of high emolument or trust. Besides the churches spared at the time of conquest no new buildings can be erected for the purposes of worship; nor can free entrance into their holy places at pleasure be refused to the Moslem. No cross must remain in view outside, nor any church-bells be rung. They must refrain from processions in the street at Easter, and other solemnities; and from any thing, in short, whether by outward symbol, word, or deed, which could be construed into rivalry, or competition with the ruling faith. Such was the so-called *Code of Omar*. En-

[1] So Jews and Christians as possessing the Bible are named in the Koran.

forced with less or greater stringency, according to the intolerance and caprice of the day, by different dynasties, it was, and (however much relaxed in certain countries) it still remains, the law of Islam. One must admire the rare tenacity of the Christian faith, which, with but scanty light and hope, held its ground through weary ages of insult and depression, and still survives to see the dawning of a brighter day.[1]

Continuing inducements in times of peace.

Such, then, was the hostile attitude of Islam militant in its early days; such the pressure brought to bear on conquered lands for its acceptance; and such the disabilities imposed upon recusant Jews and Christians. On the one hand, rapine, plunder, slavery, tribute, civil disability; on the other, security, peace, and honor. We need not be surprised that, under such constraint, conquered peoples succumbed before Islam. Nor were the temporal inducements to conversion confined to the period during which the Saracens were engaged in spreading Islam by force of arms. Let us come down a couple of centuries from the time of Mohammed, and take the reign of the tolerant and liberal-minded sovereign, Al Mamun.

[1] See *Annals*, etc., p. 213.

Evidence of Al Kindy in second century of Hegira, A. D. 830.

Among the philosophers of all creeds whom that great caliph gathered around him at Bagdad was a noble Arab of the Nestorian faith, descended from the kingly tribe of the Beni Kinda, and hence called *Al Kindy*. A friend of this Eastern Christian, himself a member of the royal family, invited Al Kindy to embrace Islam in an epistle enlarging on the distinguished rank which, in virtue of his descent, he would (if a true believer) occupy at court, and the other privileges, spiritual and material, social and conjugal, which he would enjoy. In reply the Christian wrote an apology of singular eloquence and power, throwing a flood of light on the worldly inducements which, even at that comparatively late period, abounded in a Moslem state to promote conversion to Islam. Thus Al Mamun himself, in a speech delivered before his council, characterizes certain of his courtiers accused as secret adherents of the Zoroastrian faith:

Speech of Al Mamun.

Though professing Islam, they are free from the same. This they do to be seen of me, while their convictions, I am well aware, are just the opposite of that which they profess. They belong to a class which embrace Islam, not from any love of this our faith, but thinking thereby to gain access to our court, and share in the honor, wealth, and power of the realm. They have no inward persuasion of that which they outwardly profess."[1]

Again, speaking of the various classes brought over to Islam by sordid and unworthy motives, Al Kindy says:

Converts from sordid motives.

Moreover, there are the idolatrous races—Magians and Jews—low people aspiring by the profession of Islam to raise themselves to riches and power and to form alliances with the families of the learned and honorable. There are, besides, hypocritical men of the world, who in this way obtain indulgences in the matter of marriage and concubinage which are forbidden to them by the Christian faith. Then we have the dissolute class given over wholly to the lusts of the flesh. And lastly there are those who by this means obtain a more secure and easy livelihood.[2]

Before leaving this part of our subject it may be opportune to quote a few more passages from Al Kindy, in which he contrasts the inducements that, under the military and political predominance of Islam, promoted its rapid spread, and the opposite conditions under which Christianity made progress, slow, indeed, comparatively, but sure and steady. First, he compares the Christian confessor with the Moslem "martyr:"

Al Kindy contrasts the Christian confessor with the Moslem "martyr."

The Christian confessor and the Moslem martyr.

I marvel much, he says, that ye call those *martyrs* that fall in war. Thou hast read, no doubt, in history of the followers of Christ put to

---

[1] *The Apology of Al Kindy*, written at the court of Al Mamun A. H. 215 (A. D. 830), with an essay on its age and authorship, p. 12. Smith & Elder, 1882.

[2] *Ibid.*, p. 34.

8

death in the persecutions of the kings of Persia and elsewhere. Say, now, which are the more worthy to be called martyrs, these, or thy fellows that fall fighting for the world and the power thereof? How diverse were the barbarities and kinds of death inflicted on the Christian confessors! The more they were slain the more rapidly spread the faith; in place of one sprang up a hundred. On a certain occasion, when a great multitude had been put to death, one at court said to the king, "The number of them increaseth instead of, as thou thinkest, diminishing." "How can that be?" exclaimed the king. "But yesterday," replied the courtier, "thou didst put such and such a one to death, and lo, there were converted double that number; and the people say that a man appeared to the confessors from heaven strengthening them in their last moments." Whereupon the king himself was converted. In those days men thought not their lives dear unto them. Some were transfixed while yet alive; others had their limbs cut off one after another; some were cast to the wild beasts and others burned in the fire. Such continued long to be the fate of the Christian confessors. No parallel is found thereto in any other religion; and all was endured with constancy and even with joy. One smiled in the midst of his great suffering. "Was it cold water," they asked, "that was brought unto thee?" "No," answered the sufferer, "it was one like a youth that stood by me and anointed my wounds; and that made me smile, for the pain forthwith departed."

Now tell me seriously, my friend, which of the two hath the best claim to be called a *martyr*, "slain in the ways of the Lord:" he who surrendereth his life rather than renounce his faith; who, when it is said, Fall down and worship the sun and moon, or the idols of silver and gold, work of men's hands, instead of the true God, refuseth, choosing rather to give up life, abandon wealth, and forego even wife and family; or he that goeth forth, ravaging and laying waste, plundering and spoiling, slaying the men, carrying away their children into captivity, and ravishing their wives and maidens in his unlawful embrace, and then shall call it "Jehad in the ways of the Lord!" . . . And not content therewith, instead of humbling thyself before the Lord, and seeking pardon for the crime, thou sayest of such a one slain in the war that "he hath earned paradise," and thou namest him "a martyr in the ways of the Lord!"[1]

And again, contrasting the spread of Islam, "its rattling quiver and its glittering sword," with the silent progress of Christianity, our apologist, after dwelling on the teaching and the miracles of the apostles, writes:

They published their message by means of these miracles; and thus great and powerful kings and philosophers and learned men and judges of the earth hearkened unto them, without lash or rod, with neither sword nor spear, nor the advantages of birth or "Helpers;"[2] with no wisdom of this world, or eloquence or power of language, or subtlety of reason; with no worldly inducement, nor yet again with any relaxation of the moral law, but simply at the voice of truth enforced by miracles beyond the power of man to show. And so there came over to them the kings and great ones of the earth. And the philosophers abandoned their systems, with all their wisdom and learning, and betook them to a saintly life, giving up the delights of this world together with their old-established usages, and became followers of a company of poor men, fishers and publicans, who had neither name nor rank nor any claim other than that they were obedient to the command of the Messiah—he that gave them power to do such wonderful works.[3]

The apostles compared with the chiefs of Islam.

And yet once more, comparing the apostles with the military chiefs of Islam, Al Kindy proceeds:

After the descent of the Holy Ghost and the gift of tongues the apostles separated each to the country to which he was called. They

---

[1] *Apology*, p. 47, *et. seq.*

[2] Alluding to the "*Ansar*," or mortal "Helpers" of Mohammed at Medina. Throughout, the apologist, it will be observed, is drawing a contrast with the means used for the spread of Islam. [3] *Apology*, p. 16.

wrote out in every tongue the holy Gospel, and the story and teaching of Christ, at the dictation of the Holy Ghost. So the nations drew near unto them, believing their testimony; and, giving up the world and their false beliefs, they embraced the Christian faith as soon as ever the dawn of truth and the light of the good tidings broke in upon them. Distinguishing the true from the false, and error from the right direction, they embraced the Gospel and held it fast without doubt or wavering, when they saw the wonderful works and signs of the apostles, and their lives and conversation set after the holy and beautiful example of our Saviour, the traces whereof remain even unto the present day. . . . How different this from the life of thy Master (Mohammed) and his companions, who ceased not to go forth in battle and rapine, to smite with the sword, to seize the little ones, and ravish the wives and maidens, plundering and laying waste, and carrying the people into captivity. And thus they continue unto this present day, inciting men to these evil deeds, even as it is told of Omar the Caliph. "If one among you," said he, "hath a heathen neighbor and is in need, let him seize and sell him." And many such things they say and teach. Look now at the lives of Simon and Paul, who went about healing the sick and raising the dead, by the name of Christ our Lord; and mark the contrast.[1]

Such are the conclusions of a native of Chaldea.

Such are the reflections of one who lived at a Mohammedan court, and who, moreover, flourishing as he did a thousand years ago, was sufficiently near the early spread of Islam to be able to contrast what he saw and heard and read of the causes of its success with those of the Gospel, and had the courage to confess the same.

Apart, now, from the outward and extraneous aids

[1] *Apology*, p. 57.

given to Islam by the sword and by the civil arm I will inquire for a moment what natural effect the teaching of Islam itself had in attracting or repelling mankind. I do not now speak of any power contained in the truths it inculcated to convert to Islam by the rousing and quickening of spiritual impulses; for that lies beyond my present purpose, which is to inquire whether there is not in material causes and secular motives enough in themselves to account for success. I speak rather of the effect of the indulgences granted by Islam, on the one hand, as calculated to attract; and of the restraints imposed and sacrifices required, on the other, as calculated to repel. How far, in fact, did there exist inducements or hinderances to its adoption inherent in the religion itself?

Hinderances or inducements inherent in the faith itself.

What may be regarded as the most constant and irksome of the obligations of Islam is the duty of prayer, which must be observed at stated intervals, five times every day, with the contingent ceremony of lustration. The rite consists of certain forms and passages to be repeated with prescribed series of prostrations and genuflexions. These must be repeated at the right times—but anywhere, in the house or by the way-

Requirements of Islam: prayer.

side, as well as in the mosque; and the ordinance is obligatory in whatever state of mind the worshiper may be, or however occupied. As the appointed hour comes round the Moslem is bound to turn aside to pray—so much so that in Central Asia we read of the police driving the backward worshiper by the lash to discharge the duty. Thus, with the mass of Mussulmans, the obligation becomes a mere formal ceremony, and one sees it performed anywhere and every-where by the whole people, like any social custom, as a matter of course. No doubt there are exceptions; but with the multitude it does not involve the irksomeness of a spiritual service, and so it sits lightly on high and low. The Friday prayers should as a rule be attended in the mosque; but neither need there be much devotion there; and, once performed, the rest of the day is free for pleasure or for business.[1]

Prohibition of wine, games of chance, and usury.

The prohibition of wine is a restriction which was severely felt in the early days of the faith; but it was not long before the universal sentiment (though eluded

[1] I am not here comparing the value of these observances with those of other religions. I am inquiring only how far the obligations of Islam may be held to involve hardship or sacrifice such as might have retarded the progress of Islam by rendering it on its first introduction unpopular.

in some quarters) supported it. The embargo upon games of chance was certainly unpopular; and the prohibition of the receipt of interest was also an important limitation, tending as it did to shackle the freedom of mercantile speculation; but they have been partially evaded on various pretexts. The fast throughout the month of Ramzan was a severer test; but even this lasts only during the day; and at night, from sunset till dawn, all restrictions are withdrawn, not only in respect of food, but of all otherwise lawful gratifications.[1]

Fast of Ramzan.

There is nothing, therefore, in the requirements and ordinances of Islam, excepting the fast, that is very irksome to humanity, or which, as involving any material sacrifice, or the renunciation of the pleasures or indulgences of life, should lead a man of the world to hesitate in embracing the new faith.

Little that is unpopular in these ordinances.

On the other hand, the license allowed by the Koran between the sexes—at least in favor of the male sex—is so wide that for such as have the means and the desire to take advantage of it there need be no limit whatever to sexual indulgence. It is true

Indulgences allowed in the matter of wives and concubines.

[1] See Sura ii, v. 88.

that adultery is punishable by death and fornication with stripes. But then the Koran gives the believer permission to have four wives at a time. And he may exchange them—that is, he may divorce them at pleasure, taking others in their stead.[1] And, as if this were not license enough, the divine law permits the believer to consort with all female slaves whom he may be the master of—such, namely, as have been taken in war, or have been acquired by gift or purchase. These he may receive into his harem instead of wives, or in addition to them; and without any limit of number or restraint whatever he is at liberty to cohabit with them.

Polygamy, concubinage, and divorce. Practice at the rise of Islam.

A few instances taken at random will enable the reader to judge how the indulgences thus allowed by the religion were taken advantage of in the early days of Islam. In the great plague which devastated Syria seven years after the prophet's death Khalid, the Sword of God, lost *forty* sons. Abdal Rahman, one of the "companions" of Mohammed, had issue by sixteen wives, not counting slave-girls.[2] Moghira

[1] Sura iv, 18. "Exchange" is the word used in the Koran.

[2] Each of his widows had 100,000 golden pieces left her. *Life of Mohammed*, p. 171.

ibn Shoba, another "companion," and governor of Kufa and Bussorah, had in his harem eighty consorts, free and servile. Coming closer to the Prophet's household, we find that Mohammed himself at one period had in his harem no fewer than nine wives and two slave-girls. Of his grandson Hasan we read that his vagrant passion gained for him the unenviable sobriquet of *The Divorcer*; for it was only by continually divorcing his consorts that he could harmonize his craving for fresh nuptials with the requirements of the divine law, which limited the number of his free wives to four. We are told that, as a matter of simple caprice, he exercised the power of divorce seventy (according to other traditions ninety) times. When the leading men complained to Aly of the licentious practice of his son his only reply was that the remedy lay in their own hands, of refusing Hasan their daughters altogether.[1] Such are the material inducements, the "works of the flesh," which Islam makes lawful to its votaries, and which promoted thus its early spread.

Descending now to modern times, we still find that

[1] "These divorced wives were irrespective of his concubines or slave-girls, upon the number and variety of whom there was no limit or check whatever."—*Annals*, p. 418.

this sexual license is taken advantage of more or less in different countries and conditions of society. The following examples are simply meant as showing to what excess it is possible for the believer to carry these indulgences, *under the sanction of his religion.*

Practice in modern times.

The Malays of Penang.

Of the Malays in Penang it was written not very long ago: "Young men of thirty to thirty-five years of age may be met with who have had from fifteen to twenty wives, and children by several of them. These women have been divorced, married others, and had children by them." Regarding Egypt, Lane tells us: "I have heard of men who have been in the habit of marrying a new wife almost every month."[1] Burkhardt speaks of an Arab forty-five years old who had had fifty wives, "so that he must have divorced two wives and married two fresh ones on the average every year."

Lane's testimony concerning Egypt.

The princess of Bhopal's account of Mecca.

And not to go further than the sacred city of Mecca, the late reigning princess of Bhopal, in central India, herself an orthodox follower

[1] Lane adds: "There are many men in this country who, in the course of ten years, have married as many as twenty, thirty, or more wives; and women not far advanced in age have been wives to a dozen or more husbands successively." Note that all this is entirely within the religious sanction.

of the Prophet, after making the pilgrimage of the holy places, writes thus:

> Women frequently contract as many as ten marriages, and those who have only been married twice are few in number. If a woman sees her husband growing old, or if she happen to admire any one else, she goes to the Shereef (the spiritual and civil head of the holy city), and after having settled the matter with him she puts away her husband and takes to herself another, who is, perhaps, good-looking and rich. In this way a marriage seldom lasts more than a year or two.

And of slave-girls the same high and impartial authority, still writing of the holy city and of her fellow-Moslems, tells us:

> Some of the women (African and Georgian girls) are taken in marriage; and after that, on being sold again, they receive from their masters a divorce, and are sold in their houses—that is to say, they are sent to the purchaser from their master's house on receipt of payment, and are not exposed for sale in the slave-market. They are only *married* when purchased for the first time. . . . When the poorer people buy (female) slaves they keep them for themselves, and change them every year as one would replace old things by new; but the women who have children are not sold.[1]

---

[1] *Pilgrimage to Mecca*, by her highness the reigning Begum of Bhopal, translated by Mrs. W. Osborne (1870), pp. 82, 88. Slave-girls cannot be *married* until freed by their masters. What her highness tells of women *divorcing* their husbands is of course entirely *ultra vires*, and shows how the laxity of conjugal relations allowed to the male sex has extended itself to the female also, and that in a city where, if anywhere, we should have expected to find the law observed.

Islam sanctions a license between the sexes which Christianity forbids.

What I desire to make clear is the fact that such things may be practiced *with the sanction* of the Scripture which the Moslem holds to be divine, and that these same indulgences have from the first existed as inducements which helped materially to forward the spread of the faith. I am very far, indeed, from implying that excessive indulgence in polygamy is the universal state of Moslem society. Happily this is not the case. There are not only individuals, but tribes and districts, which, either from custom or preference, voluntarily restrict the license given them in the Koran; while the natural influence of the family, even in Moslem countries, has an antiseptic tendency that often itself tends greatly to neutralize the evil.[1] Nor am I seeking to institute any contrast be-

[1] In India, for example, there are Mohammedan races among whom monogamy, as a rule, prevails by custom, and individuals exercising their right of polygamy are looked upon with disfavor. On the other hand, we meet occasionally with men who aver that rather against their will (as they will sometimes rather amusingly say) they have been forced by custom or family influence to add by polygamy to their domestic burdens. In Mohammedan countries, however, when we hear of a man confining himself to *one wife*, it does not necessarily follow that he has no slaves to consort with in his harem. I may remark that slave-girls have by Mohammedan laws no conjugal rights whatever, but are like playthings, at the absolute discretion of their master.

tween the morals at large of Moslem countries and the rest of the world. If Christian nations are (as with shame it must be confessed) in some strata of society immoral, it is in the teeth of their divine law. And the restrictions of that law are calculated, and in the early days of Christianity did tend, in point of fact, *to deter men* devoted to the indulgences of the flesh from embracing the faith.[1] The religion of Mohammed, on the other hand, gives direct sanction to the sexual indulgences we have been speaking of. Thus it panders to the lower instincts of humanity and makes its spread the easier. In direct opposition to the precepts of Christianity it "makes provision for the flesh to fulfill the lusts thereof." Hence Islam has been well called by its own votaries the *Easy Way*. Once more, to quote Al Kindy:

The laws of Christianity deter men from carnal indulgences.

Islam the "Easy Way."

Thou invitest me (says our apologist to his friend) into the "Easy way of faith and practice." Alas, alas! for our Saviour in the Gospel telleth us, "When ye have done all that ye are commanded, say, We are unprofitable servants; we have but done that which was commanded us." Where then is our merit? The same Lord Jesus saith,

---

[1] The case of the Corinthian offender is much in point, as showing how the strict discipline of the Church must have availed to make Christianity unpopular with the mere worldling.

"How strait is the road which leadeth unto life, and how few they be that walk therein! How wide the gate that leadeth to destruction, and how many there be that go in thereat!" Different this, my friend, from the comforts of thy wide and easy gate, and the facilities for enjoying, as thou wouldst have me, the pleasures offered by thy faith in wives and damsels![1]

---

[1] *Apology*, p. 51. I repeat, that in the remarks I have made under this head, no comparison is sought to be drawn betwixt the morality of nominally Christian and Moslem peoples. On this subject I may be allowed to quote from what I have said elsewhere: "The Moslem advocate will urge . . . the social evil as the necessary result of inexorable monogamy. The Koran not only denounces any illicit laxity between the sexes in the severest terms, but exposes the transgressor to condign punishment. For this reason, and because the conditions of what is licit are so accommodating and wide, a certain negative virtue (it can hardly be called continence or chastity) pervades Mohammedan society, in contrast with which the gross and systematic immorality in certain parts of every European community may be regarded by the Christian with shame and confusion. In a purely Mohammedan land, however low may be the general level of moral feeling, the still lower depths of fallen humanity are unknown. The 'social evil' and intemperance, prevalent in Christian lands, are the strongest weapons in the armory of Islam. We point, and justly, to the higher morality and civilization of those who do observe the precepts of the Gospel, to the stricter unity and virtue which cement the family, and to the elevation of the sex; but in vain, while the example of our great cities, and too often of our representatives abroad, belies the argument. And yet the argument is sound. For, in proportion as Christianity exercises her legitimate influence, vice and intemperance will wane and vanish, and the higher morality pervade the whole body; whereas in Islam the deteriorating influences of polygamy, divorce, and concubinage have been stereotyped for all time."—*The Koran: its Composition and Teaching, and the Testimony it bears to the Holy Scriptures*, p. 60.

Laxity among nominal Christians.

II.

WHY THE SPREAD OF ISLAM WAS STAYED.

Islam stationary in area, and in civilization retrograde.

HAVING thus traced the rapid early spread of Islam to its proper source, I proceed to the remaining topics, namely, the causes which have checked its further extension, and those likewise which have depressed the followers of this religion in the scale of civilization. I shall take the former first—just remarking here, in respect of the latter, that the depression of Islam is itself one of the causes which retard the expansion of the faith.

The Arabs ceased, in second century, to be a crusading force.

As the first spread of Islam was due to the sword, so when the sword was sheathed Islam ceased to spread. The apostles and missionaries of Islam were, as we have seen, the martial tribes of Arabia—that is to say, the grand military force organized by Omar, and by him launched upon the surrounding nations. Gorged with the plunder of the world, these began, after a time, to settle on their lees and to mingle with the ordinary population. So soon as this came to pass they lost the fiery zeal which at the first had made them irresistible. By the second and third centuries the Arabs had disappeared as the standing army of the caliphate, or, in other words, as a body set apart for the dissemination of the faith. The crusading spirit, indeed, ever and anon burst forth—and it still bursts forth, as opportunity offers—simply for the reason that this spirit pervades the Koran, and is ingrained in the creed. But with the special agency created and maintained during the first ages for the spread of Islam the incentive of crusade ceased as a distinctive missionary spring of action, and degenerated into the common lust of conquest which we meet with in the world at large.

With cessation of conquest, Islam ceased to spread.

The extension of Islam, depending upon military success, stopped wherever that was checked. The religion advanced or retired, speaking broadly, as the armed predominance made head or retroceded. Thus the tide of Moslem victory, rushing along the coast of Africa, extinguished the seats of European civilization on the Mediterranean, overwhelmed Spain, and was rapidly advancing north, when the onward wave was stemmed at Tours; and as with the arms, the faith also of Islam was driven back into Spain and bounded by the Pyrenees. So, likewise, the hold which the religion seized both of Spain and Sicily came to an end with Mussulman defeat. It is true that when once long and firmly rooted, as in India and China, Islam may survive the loss of military power, and even flourish. But it is equally true that in no single country has Islam been planted, nor has it anywhere materially spread, saving under the banner of the Crescent or the political ascendency of some neighboring State. Accordingly, we find that, excepting some barbarous zones in Africa which have been raised thereby a step above the groveling level of fetichism, the faith has in modern times made no advance worth mentioning.[1]

Alleged progress of Islam in Africa.

[1] Much loose assertion has been made regarding the progress of Islam in Africa; but I have found no proof of it apart from armed, political, or trading influence, dogged too often by the slave-trade; to a great extent a social rather than a religious movement, and raising the fetich tribes (haply without intemperance) into a somewhat higher stage of semi-barbarism. I have met nothing which would touch the argument in the text. The following is the testimony of Dr. Koelle, the best possible witness on the subject:

"It is true the Mohammedan nations in the interior of Africa, namely, the Bornuese, Mandengas, Pulas, etc., invited by the weak and defenseless condition of the surrounding negro tribes, still occasionally make conquests, and after subduing a tribe of pagans, by almost exterminating its male population and committing the most horrible atrocities, impose upon those that remain the creed of Islam; but keeping in view the whole of the Mohammedan world this fitful

From the Jewish and Christian religions there has (again speaking broadly) been no secession whatever to Islam since the wave of Saracen victory was stayed, excepting by the force of arms. Even in the palmy days of the Abbasside caliphs, our apologist could challenge his adversary to produce a single conversion otherwise than by reason of some powerful material inducement. Here is his testimony:

Al Kindy's challenge to produce a Christian convert to Islam apart from material inducements.

> Now tell me, hast thou ever seen, my Friend, (the Lord be gracious unto thee!) or ever heard of a single person of sound mind—any one of learning and experience, and acquainted with the Scriptures, renouncing Christianity otherwise than for some worldly object to be reached only through thy religion, or for some gratification withheld by the faith of Jesus? Thou wilt find none. For, excepting the tempted ones, all continue steadfast in their faith, secure under our most gracious sovereign, in the profession of their own religion.[1]

---

activity reminds one only of these green branches sometimes seen on trees, already, and for long, decayed at the core from age."—*Food for Reflection*, p. 37.

[1] *Apology*, p. 34.

III.

LOW POSITION OF ISLAM IN THE SCALE OF CIVILIZATION.

Social and intellectual depression.

I PASS on to consider why Mohammedan nations occupy so low a position, halting as almost every-where they do, in the march of social and intellectual development.

Islam intended for the Arabs.

The reason is not far to find. Islam was meant for Arabia, not for the world; for the Arabs of the seventh century, not for the Arabs of all time; and being such, and nothing more, its claim of divine origin renders change or development impossible. It has within itself neither the germ of natural growth nor the lively spring of adaptation. Mohammed declared himself a prophet to the Arabs;[1] and however much in his later days he may have contemplated the reformation of other religions beyond the Peninsula, or the further spread of his own (which is doubtful), still the rites and ceremonies, the customs and the laws enjoined upon his people, were suitable

[1] *Annals*, pp. 61, 224.

(if suitable at all) for the Arabs of that day, and in many respects for them alone. Again, the code containing these injunctions, social and ceremonial, as well as doctrinal and didactic, is embodied with every particularity of detail, as part of the divine law, in the Koran; and so defying, as sacrilege, all human touch, it stands unalterable forever. From the stiff and rigid shroud in which it is thus swathed the religion of Mohammed cannot emerge. It has no plastic power beyond that exercised in its earliest days. Hardened now and inelastic, it can neither adapt itself nor yet shape its votaries, nor even suffer them to shape themselves to the varying circumstances, the wants and developments, of mankind.

Wants the faculty of adaptation.

We may judge of the local and inflexible character of the faith from one or two of its ceremonies. To perform the pilgrimage to Mecca and Mount Arafat, with the slaying of victims at Mina, and the worship of the Kaaba, is an ordinance obligatory (with the condition only that they have the means) on all believers, who are bound to make the journey even from the furthest ends of the earth—an ordinance intelligible enough in a local worship, but unmeaning and impracticable when re-

Local ceremonies: pilgrimage.

Fast of Ramzan.

quired of a world-wide religion. The same may be said of the fast of Ramzan. It is prescribed in the Koran to be observed by all with undeviating strictness during the whole day, from earliest dawn till sunset throughout the month, with specified exemptions for the sick and penalties for every occasion on which it is broken. The command, imposed thus with an iron rule on male and female, young and old, operates with excessive inequality in different seasons, lands, and climates. However suitable to countries near the equator, where the variations of day and night are immaterial, the fast becomes intolerable to those who are far removed either toward the north or the south; and still closer to the poles, where night merges into day and day into night, impracticable. Again, with the lunar year (itself an institution divinely imposed), the month of Ramzan travels in the third of a century from month to month over the whole cycle of a year. The fast was established at a time when Ramzan fell in winter, and the change of season was probably not foreseen by the Prophet. But the result is one which, under some conditions of time and place, involves the greatest hardship. For when the fast comes round to summer the trial in a sultry climate, like that of the burning Indian plains, of passing the whole day without a morsel of bread or a drop of water becomes to many the occasion of intense suffering. Such is the effect of the Arabian legislator's attempt at circumstantial legislation in matters of religious ceremonial.

Political and social depression owing to relations between the sexes.

Nearly the same is the case with all the religious obligations of Islam, prayer, lustration, etc. But although the minuteness of detail with which these are enjoined tends toward that jejune and formal worship which we witness every-where in Moslem lands, still there is nothing in these observances themselves which (religion apart) should lower the social condition of Mohammedan populations and prevent their emerging from that normal state of semi-barbarism and uncivilized depression in which we find all Moslem peoples. For the cause of this we must look elsewhere; and it may be recognized, without doubt, in the relations established by the Koran between the sexes. Polygamy, divorce, servile concubinage, and the veil are at the root of Moslem decadence.

Depression of the female sex.

In respect of married life the condition allotted by the Koran to woman is that of an inferior dependent creature, destined only for the service of her master, liable to be cast adrift without the assignment of a single reason or the notice of a single hour. While the husband possesses the power of a divorce—absolute, immediate, unquestioned—no privilege of a corresponding nature has been reserved for the wife. She hangs on, however unwilling, neglected, or superseded, the perpetual slave of her lord, if such be his will. When actually divorced she can, indeed, claim her dower—her *hire*, as it is called in the too plain language of the Koran; but the knowledge that the wife can make this claim is at the best a miserable security against capricious taste; and in the case of bondmaids even that imperfect check is wanting. The power of divorce is not the only power that may be exercised by the tyrannical husband. Authority to *confine* and to *beat* his wives is distinctly vested in his discretion.[1] "Thus restrained, secluded, degraded, the mere minister of enjoyment, liable at the caprice or passion of the moment to be turned adrift, it would be hard to say that the position of a wife was improved by the code of Mohammed."[2] Even if the privilege of divorce and marital tyranny be not exercised, the knowledge of its existence as a potential right must

Divorce.

[1] Sura iv, v. 33. [2] *Life of Mohammed*, p. 348.

tend to abate the self-respect, and in like degree to weaken the influence of the sex, impairing thus the ameliorating and civilizing power which she was meant to exercise upon mankind. And the evil has been stereotyped by the Koran for all time.

Principal Fairbairn on home-life under Islam.

I must quote one more passage from Principal Fairbairn on the lowering influence of Moslem domestic life:

The God of Mohammed . . . "spares the sins the Arab loves. A religion that does not purify the home cannot regenerate the race; one that depraves the home is certain to deprave humanity. Motherhood is to be sacred if manhood is to be honorable. Spoil the wife of sanctity and for the man the sanctities of life have perished. And so it has been with Islam. It has reformed and lifted savage tribes; it has depraved and barbarized civilized nations. At the root of its fairest culture a worm has ever lived that has caused its blossoms soon to wither and die. Were Mohammed the hope of man, then his state were hopeless; before him could only be retrogression, tyranny, and despair."[1]

Demoralizing influence of servile concubinage.

Still worse is the influence of servile concubinage. The following is the evidence of a shrewd and able observer in the East:

All zenana life must be bad for men at all stages of their existence. . . . In youth it must be ruin to be petted and spoiled by a company of submissive slave-girls. In manhood it is no less an evil that when a man enters into private life his affections should be put up to auc-

[1] *The City of God*, p. 97. Hodder & Stoughton, 1883.

tion among foolish, fond competitors full of mutual jealousies and slanders. We are not left entirely to conjecture as to the effect of female influence on home-life when it is exerted under these unenlightened and demoralizing conditions. That is plainly an element *lying at the root of all the most important features that differentiate progress from stagnation.*[1]

Deteriorating influence of relations established between the sexes.

Such are the institutions which gnaw at the root of Islam and prevent the growth of freedom and civilization. "By these the unity of the household is fatally broken and the purity and virtue of the family tie weakened; the vigor of the dominant classes is sapped; the body politic becomes weak and languid, excepting for intrigues, and the throne itself liable to fall a prey to a doubtful or contested succession"[2]—contested by the progeny of the various rivals crowded into the royal harem. From the palace downward polygamy and servile concubinage lower the moral tone, loosen the ties of domestic life, and hopelessly depress the people.

The veil.

Nor is the veil, albeit under the circumstances a necessary precaution, less detrimental, though in a different way, to the interests of Moslem society. This strange custom owes its

[1] *The Turks in India*, by H. G. Keene, C.S.I. Allen & Co., 1879.

[2] *Annals*, etc., p. 457.

origin to the Prophet's jealous temperament. It is forbidden in the Koran for women to appear unveiled before any member of the other sex with the exception of certain near relatives of specified propinquity.[1] And this law, coupled with other restrictions of the kind, has led to the imposition of the *boorka* or *purdah* (the dress which conceals the person and the veil) and to the greater or less seclusion of the harem and zenana.

Society vitiated by the withdrawal of the female sex.

This ordinance and the practices flowing from it must survive, more or less, so long as the Koran remains the rule of faith. It may appear at first sight a mere negative evil, a social custom comparatively harmless; but in truth it has a more debilitating effect upon the Moslem race perhaps than any thing else, for by it *woman is totally withdrawn from her proper place in the social circle.* She may, indeed, in the comparatively laxer license of some lands be seen flitting along the streets or driving in her carriage; but even so it is like one belonging to another world, veiled, shrouded, and cut

[1] See Sura xxxiv, v. 32. The excepted relations are: "Husbands, fathers, husbands' fathers, sons, husbands' sons, brothers, brothers' sons, sisters' sons, the captives which their right hands possess, such men as attend them and have no need of women, or children below the age of puberty."

off from intercourse with those around her. Free only in the retirement of her own secluded apartments, she is altogether shut out from her legitimate sphere in the duties and enjoyments of life. But the blight on the sex itself from this unnatural regulation, sad as it is, must be regarded as a minor evil. The mischief extends beyond her. The tone and framework of society as it came from the Maker's hands are altered, damaged, and deteriorated. From the veil there flows this double injury. The bright, refining, softening influence of woman is withdrawn from the outer world, and social life, wanting the gracious influences of the female sex, becomes, as we see throughout Moslem lands, forced, hard, unnatural, and morose. Moreover, the Mohammedan nations, for all purposes of common elevation and for all efforts of philanthropy and liberty, are (as they live in public and beyond the inner recesses of their homes) but a truncated and imperfect exhibition of humanity. They are wanting in one of its constituent parts, the better half, the humanizing and the softening element. And it would be against the nature of things to suppose that the body, thus shorn and mutilated, can possess in itself the virtue and power of progress,

Mohammedan society, thus truncated, incapable of progress.

The defects of Mohammedan society.

reform, and elevation. The link connecting the family with social and public life is detached, and so neither is *en rapport*, as it should be, with the other. Reforms fail to find entrance into the family or to penetrate the domestic soil where alone they could take root, grow into the national mind, live, and be perpetuated. Under such conditions the seeds of civilization refuse to germinate. No real growth is possible in free and useful institutions, nor any permanent and healthy force in those great movements which elsewhere tend to uplift the masses and elevate mankind. There may, it is true, be some advance, from time to time, in science and in material prosperity; but the social groundwork for the same is wanting, and the people surely relapse into the semi-barbarism forced upon them by an ordinance which is opposed to the best instincts of humanity. Sustained progress becomes impossible. Such is the outcome of an attempt to improve upon nature and banish woman, the help-meet of man, from the position assigned by God to her in the world.

Yet the veil necessary under existing circumstances.

At the same time I am not prepared to say that in view of the laxity of the conjugal relations inherent in the institutions of Islam some such social check as that of the veil (apart from the power to confine and castigate) is not needed for the repression of license and the maintenance of outward decency. There is too much reason to apprehend that free social intercourse might otherwise be dangerous to morality under the code of Mohammed, and with the example before men and women of the early worthies of Islam. So long as the sentiments and habits of the Moslem world remain as they are some remedial or preventive measure of the kind seems indispensable. But the peculiarity of the Mussulman polity, as we have seen, is such that the sexual laws and institutions which call for restrictions of the kind as founded on the Koran are incapable of change; they must co-exist with the faith itself, and last while it lasts. So long, then, as this polity prevails the depression of woman, as well as her exclusion from the social circle, must injure the health and vitality of the body politic, impair its purity and grace, paralyze vigor, retard progress in the direction of freedom, philanthropy, and moral elevation, and generally perpetuate the normal state of Mohammedan peoples, as one of semi-barbarism.

To recapitulate, we have seen:

Recapitulation.

First. That Islam was propagated mainly by the sword. With the tide of conquest the religion went forward; where conquest was arrested made no advance beyond; and at the withdrawal of the Moslem arms the faith also commonly retired.

Second. The inducements, whether material or spiritual, to embrace Islam have proved insufficient of themselves (speaking broadly) to spread the faith, in the absence of the sword, and without the influence of the political or secular arm.

Third. The ordinances of Islam, those especially having respect to the female sex, have induced an inherent weakness, which depresses the social system and retards its progress.

Contrast with Christianity.

If the reader should have followed me in the argument by which these conclusions have been reached the contrast with the Christian faith has no doubt been suggesting itself at each successive step.

Christianity not propagated by force.

Christianity, as Al Kindy has so forcibly put it, gained a firm footing in the world without the sword, and without any aid whatever from the secular arm. So far from having the countenance of the State it triumphed in spite of opposition, persecution, and discouragement. "My kingdom," said Jesus, "is not of this world. If my kingdom were of this world, then would my servants fight that I should not be delivered to the Jews; but now is my kingdom not from hence. . . . For this end came I into the world, that I should bear witness to the truth. Every one that is of the truth, heareth my voice."[1]

Nor by worldly inducements.

The religion itself, in its early days, offered no worldly attractions or indulgences. It was not, like Islam, an "easy way." Whether in withdrawal from social observances deeply tainted with idolatry, the refusal to participate in sacrificial ceremonies insisted on by the rulers, or in the renunciation of indulgences inconsistent with a saintly life, the Christian profession required self-denial at every step.

Adaptive principles and plastic faculty of Christianity.

But otherwise the teaching of Christianity nowhere interfered with the civil institutions of the countries into which it penetrated or with any social customs or practices that were not in themselves immoral or idolatrous. It did not, indeed, neglect to guide the Christian life. But it did so by the enunciation of principles and rules of wide and far-reaching application. These, no less than the injunctions of the Koran, served amply for

[1] John xviii, 36, 37.

the exigencies of the day. But they have done a vast deal more. They have proved themselves capable of adaptation to the most advanced stages of social development and intellectual elevation. And, what is infinitely more, it may be claimed for the lessons embodied in the Gospel that they have been themselves promotive, if indeed they have not been the immediate cause, of all the most important reforms and philanthropies that now prevail in Christendom. The principles thus laid down contained germs endowed with the power of life and growth which, expanding and flourishing, slowly it may be, but surely, have at the last borne the fruits we see.

Examples: slavery.

Take, for example, the institution of slavery. It prevailed in the Roman Empire at the introduction of Christianity, as it did in Arabia at the rise of Islam. In the Moslem code, as we have seen, the practice has been perpetuated. Slavery must be held permissible so long as the Koran is taken to be the rule of faith. The divine sanction thus impressed upon the institution, and the closeness with which by law and custom it intermingles with social and domestic life, make it impossible for any Mohammedan people to impugn slavery as contrary to sound morality or for any body of loyal believers to advocate its abolition upon the ground of principle. There are, moreover, so many privileges and gratifications accruing to the higher classes from its maintenance that (excepting under the strong pressure of European diplomacy) no sincere and hearty effort can be expected from the Moslem race in the suppression of the inhuman traffic, the horrors of which, as pursued by Moslem slave-traders, their Prophet would have been the first to denounce. Look now at the wisdom with which the Gospel treats the institution. It is nowhere in so many words proscribed, for that would, under the circumstances, have led to the abnegation of relative duties and the disruption of society. It is accepted as a prevailing institution recognized by the civil powers. However desirable freedom might be, slavery was not inconsistent with the Christian profession: "Art thou called being a servant? care not for it: but if thou mayest be made free, use it rather." 1 Cor. vii, 21. The duty of obedience to his master is enjoined upon the slave, and the duty of mildness and urbanity toward his slave is enjoined upon the master. But with all this was laid the seed which grew into emancipation. "*Our Father*," gave the key-note of freedom. "Ye are *all* the children of God by faith in Christ Jesus." "There is neither bond nor free, Gal. iii, 26, 28. . . . for ye are all one in Christ Jesus." 1 Cor. vii, 22. "He that is called in the Lord, being a servant, is the Lord's freeman." The converted slave is to be received "not now as a servant, but above a servant, a brother beloved." Philemon 16. The seed has borne its proper harvest. Late in time, no doubt, but by a sure and certain development, the grand truth of the equality of the human race, and the right of every man and woman to freedom of thought and (within reasonable limit of law) to freedom of action, has triumphed; and it has triumphed through the Spirit and the precepts inculcated by the Gospel eighteen hundred years ago. Nor is it otherwise with the relations established between the sexes.

Relations between the sexes.

Polygamy, divorce, and concubinage with bondmaids have been perpetuated, as we have seen, by Islam for all time; and the ordinances connected therewith have given rise, in the laborious task of defining the conditions and limits of what is lawful, to a mass of prurient casuistry defiling the books of Mohammedan law. Contrast with this our Saviour's words, Matt. xix, 4. "*He which made them at the beginning made them male and female. . . . What there-*

fore God hath joined together let not man put asunder." From which simple utterance have resulted monogamy and (in the absence of adultery) the indissolubility of the marriage bond. While in respect of conjugal duties we have such large, but sufficiently intelligible, commands as "to render due benevolence," whereby, while the obligations of the marriage state are maintained, Christianity is saved from the impurities which, in expounding the ordinances of Mohammed, surround the sexual ethics of Islam, and cast so foul a stain upon its literature.

1 Cor. vii, 3.

Take, again, the place of woman in the world. We need no injunction of the veil or the harem. As the temples of the Holy Ghost, the body is to be kept undefiled, and every one is "to possess his vessel in sanctification and honor." Men are to treat "the elder women as mothers; the younger as sisters, with all purity." Women are to "adorn themselves in modest apparel, with shamefacedness and sobriety." These, and such like maxims embrace the whole moral fitness of the several relations and duties which they define. They are adapted for all ages of time and for all conditions of men. They are capable of being taken

Elevation of woman.

1 Thess. iv, 4.

1 Tim. v, 2.

1 Tim. ii, 9.

by every individual for personal guidance, according to his own sense of propriety, and they can be accommodated by society at large with a due reference to the habits and customs of the day. The attempt of Mohammed to lay down, with circumstantial minuteness, the position of the female sex, the veiling of her person, and her withdrawal from the gaze of man, has resulted in seclusion and degradation; while the spirit of the Gospel, and injunctions like that of "giving honor to the wife as to the weaker vessel," have borne the fruit of woman's elevation, and have raised her to the position of influence, honor, and equality which (notwithstanding the marital superiority of the husband in the ideal of a Christian family) she now occupies in the social scale.

1 Pet. iii, 7.

In the type of Mussulman government which (though not laid down in the Koran) is founded upon the spirit of the faith and the precedent of the Prophet the civil is indissolubly blended with the spiritual authority, to the detriment of religious liberty and political progress. The *Ameer*, or commander of the faithful, should, as in the early times, so also in all ages, be the *Imam*, or religious chief; and as such he should preside at the

Relations with the State.

weekly cathedral service. It is not a case of the Church being subject to the State, or the State being subject to the Church. Here (as we used to see in the papal domains) the Church is the State, and the State the Church. They both are one. And in this we have another cause of the backwardness and depression of Mohammedan society. Since the abolition of the temporal power in Italy we have nowhere in Christian lands any such theocratic union of Cæsar and the Church, so that secular and religious advance is left more or less unhampered; whereas in Islam the hierarchico-political constitution has hopelessly welded the secular arm with the spiritual in one common scepter, to the furthering of despotism, and elimination of the popular voice from its proper place in the concerns of State.

Christianity leaves humanity free to expand.

And so, throughout the whole range of political, religious, social, and domestic relations, the attempt made by the founder of Islam to provide for all contingencies, and to fix every thing aforehand by rigid rule and scale, has availed to cramp and benumb the free activities of life and to paralyze the natural efforts of society at healthy growth, expansion, and reform. As an author already quoted

The Koran checks progress.

has so well put it, "*The Koran has frozen Mohammedan thought; to obey it is to abandon progress.*"[1]

Is Islam suitable for any nation?

Writers have indeed been found who, dwelling upon the benefits conferred by Islam on idolatrous and savage nations, have gone so far as to hold that the religion of Mohammed may in consequence be suited to certain portions of mankind—as if the faith of Jesus might peaceably divide with it the world. But surely to acquiesce in a system which reduces the people to a dead level of social depression, despotism, and semi-barbarism would be abhorrent from the first principles of philanthropy. With the believer, who holds the Gospel to be "good tidings of great joy, *which shall be to all people*," such a notion is on higher grounds untenable; but even in view of purely secular considerations it is not only untenable, but altogether unintelligible. As I have said elsewhere:

Luke ii, 10.

The eclipse in the East, which still sheds its blight on the ancient seats of Jerome and Chrysostom, and shrouds in darkness the once bright and famous sees of Cyprian and Augustine, has been disastrous every-where to liberty and progress, equally as it has been to Christianity. And it is only as that eclipse shall pass away and the Sun of righteousness again shine forth that we can look to the nations now dominated by Islam sharing with us those secondary but

[1] Dr. Fairbairn, *Contemporary Review*, p. 865.

precious fruits of divine teaching. Then with the higher and enduring blessings which our faith bestows, but not till then, we may hope that there will follow likewise in their wake freedom and progress, and all that tends to elevate the human race.[1]

No sacrifice for sin or redemptive grace.

Although with the view of placing the argument on independent ground I have refrained from touching the peculiar doctrines of Christianity, and the inestimable benefits which flow to mankind therefrom, I may be excused, before I conclude, if I add a word regarding them. The followers of Mohammed have no knowledge of God as a *Father;* still less have they knowledge of him as "*Our* Father"—the God and Father of the Lord Jesus Christ. They acknowledge, indeed, that Jesus was a true prophet sent of God; but they deny his crucifixion and death, and they know nothing of the power of his resurrection. To those who have found redemption and peace in these the grand and distinctive truths of the Christian faith, it may be allowed to mourn over the lands in which the light of the Gospel has been quenched, and these blessings blotted out, by the material forces of Islam; where, together with civilization and liberty, Christianity has given place to gross darkness, and it is as if now

[1] *The Early Caliphate and Rise of Islam*, being the Rede Lecture for 1881, delivered before the University of Cambridge, p. 28.

"there were no more sacrifice for sins." We may, and we do, look forward with earnest expectation to the day when knowledge of salvation shall be given to these nations "by the remission of their sins, through the tender mercy of our God, whereby the Dayspring from on high hath visited us, to give light to them that sit in darkness and in the shadow of death, to guide our feet into the way of peace."

Luke i, 77–79.

Contrast between divine and human work.

But even apart from these, the special blessings of Christianity, I ask, which now of the two faiths bears, in its birth and growth, the mark of a divine hand and which the human stamp? Which looks likest the handiwork of the God of nature, who "hath laid the measures of the earth," and "hath stretched the line upon it," but not the less with an ever-varying adaptation to time and place? and which the artificial imitation?

Job xxxviii, 5.

Islam.

"As a reformer, Mohammed did indeed advance his people to a certain point, but as a prophet he left them fixed immovably at that point for all time to come. As there can be no return, so neither can there be any progress. The tree is of artificial planting. Instead of containing within itself the germ of growth and adaptation to the various requirements of time, and clime, and circumstance, expanding with the genial sunshine and the rain from heaven, it remains the same forced and stunted thing as when first planted twelve centuries ago."[1]

Christianity compared by Christ to the works of nature.

Such is Islam. Now what is Christianity? Listen to the prophetic words of the Founder himself, who compares it to the works of nature:

"*So is the kingdom of God, as if a man should cast seed into the ground;*

Mark iv, 26-28.

"*And should sleep, and rise night and day, and the seed should spring and grow up, he knoweth not how.*

"*For the earth bringeth forth fruit of herself: first the blade, then the ear, after that the full corn in the ear.*"

And again:

"*Whereunto shall we liken the kingdom of God, or with what comparison shall we compare it?*

Mark iv, 30-32.

"*It is like a grain of mustard-seed, which, when it is sown in the earth, is less than all seeds that be in the earth;*

"*But when it is sown, it groweth up and becometh greater than all herbs, and shooteth out great branches, so that the fowls of the air may lodge under the shadow of it.*"

Islam the work of man; Christianity the work of God.

Which is *nature*, and which is *art*, let the reader judge. Which bears the impress of man's hand, and which that of Him who "is wonderful in counsel, and excellent in working?"

In fine, of the Arabian it may be said:

"*Hitherto shalt thou come, but no further, and here shall thy proud waves be stayed.*"

---

[1] *The Koran*, etc., p. 65.

But of Christ:

"*His name shall endure forever: his name shall be continued as long as the sun: and men shall be blessed in him: all nations shall call him blessed.*

Psa. lxxii, 17, 8, 18, 19. "*He shall have dominion also from sea to sea, and from the river unto the ends of the earth.*

"*Blessed be the Lord God, the God of Israel, who only doeth wondrous things. And blessed be his glorious name forever: and let the whole earth be filled with his glory. Amen, and Amen.*"

THE END.